LABORATORY MANUAL TO ACCOMPANY

Security Strategies in Windows Platforms and Applications

vLAB
SOLUTIONS

JONES & BARTLETT
LEARNING

World Headquarters
Jones & Bartlett Learning
5 Wall Street
Burlington, MA 01803
978-443-5000
info@jblearning.com
www.jblearning.com

Jones & Bartlett Learning books and products are available through most bookstores and online booksellers. To contact Jones & Bartlett Learning directly, call 800-832-0034, fax 978-443-8000, or visit our website, www.jblearning.com.

This publication is designed to provide accurate and authoritative information in regard to the subject matter covered. It is sold with the understanding that the publisher is not engaged in rendering legal, accounting, or other professional service. If legal advice or other expert assistance is required, the service of a competent professional person should be sought.

Production Credits
Chief Executive Officer: Ty Field
President: James Homer
SVP, Chief Operating Officer: Don Jones, Jr.
SVP, Chief Technology Officer: Dean Fossella
SVP, Chief Marketing Officer: Alison M. Pendergast
SVP, Curriculum Solutions: Christopher Will
VP, Design and Production: Anne Spencer
VP, Manufacturing and Inventory Control: Therese Connell
Author: vLab Solutions, LLC, David Kim, President
Editorial Management: Perspectives, Inc., Phil Graham, President
Reprints and Special Projects Manager: Susan Schultz
Associate Production Editor: Tina Chen
Director of Marketing: Alisha Weisman
Senior Marketing Manager: Andrea DeFronzo
Cover Design: Anne Spencer
Composition: vLab Solutions, LLC
Cover Image: © Handy Widiyanto/ShutterStock, Inc.
Printing and Binding: Malloy, Inc.
Cover Printing: Malloy, Inc.

ISBN: 978-1-4496-4394-2

6048
Printed in the United States of America
15 14 13 12 11   10 9 8 7 6 5 4 3 2 1

Table of Contents

Current Version Date: 05/27/2011

Current Version Date: 05/27/2011

Current Version Date: 05/27/2011

Laboratory #1

Lab #1: Configure Active Directory and Implement Departmental and User Access Controls

Learning Objectives and Outcomes

Upon completing this equipment-based lab, students will be able to complete the following tasks:

- Create Windows 2008 Standard Server R2 Active Directory system administration configurations for defined departmental workgroups and users

- Create Windows 2008 Standard Server R2 global domain departmental groups and user account definitions per defined access control requirements

- Configure Windows 2008 Standard Server R2 departmental group and user folders with unique access rights per the defined access control requirements

- Access a Windows 2008 Standard Server R2 as a user and encounter errors when attempting to create data files and write them to specific folders

- Create a list of new and modified access control parameters to implement stringent security access controls per the defined requirements using Windows 2008 Standard Server R2

Required Setup and Tools

The following are **required** for this equipment-based lab:

A) A classroom workstation with at least 4GB of RAM capable of supporting the removable hard drive with the VM server farm

B) An Instructor workstation with at least 2 Gig RAM/4Gig RAM recommended that shall act as the instructor's demo lab workstation. The Instructor will display the workstation on the projector to demo the loading and configuring of the Target VMs using VMware Player

C) Student Lab workstations will use their own VM server farm and classroom workstation. VMware Player will be used to run the Target VMs and perform the equipment-based steps

NOTE: In this course only the virtual machines named 'Target2k8a' and 'Target2k8b' contained in the removable hard drive are required to perform equipment-based labs. The workstations with 4GB of RAM can support two Target VMs. Virtual machines can be Paused or Stopped when not in use in order to maximize performance. One VM at a time is recommended for a system with 2GB of RAM.

Current Version Date: 05/27/2011

The following summarizes the setup, configuration, and equipment needed to perform Lab #1:

1. Standard classroom workstation and external hard drive with Virtual server farm

2. Virtual machines required for Lab #1:

   o 'Target2k8a' > same as > "Windows2k8a"

   o 'Target2k8b' > same as > "Windows2k8b"

3. Target VM configurations are as follows:

   o Microsoft Windows 2008 Standard Server R2

   o Domain Name: corp.vlabs.local

   o Domain and Local Administrator access:

      ▪ Username: administrator

      ▪ Password: ISS316Security

'Target2k8a' Roles installed: Active Directory Services and DNS

NOTE: When performing these equipment-based labs, you can use existing drive mappings C:\\, D:\\ or create new ones as system administrator, etc.

Equipment-Based Lab #1 – Student Steps

Creating and Linking Group Policy Objects

1. Connect removable hard drive containing the Mock IT Server Farm to your workstation.

2. Login to the classroom workstation using your login credentials.

3. Power-up the "Target2k8a" virtual machine using VMware Player.

4. Log into "Target2k8a" as administrator with the following credentials:

   a. Username: administrator

   b. Password: ISS316Security

5. Launch GPMC on "Target2k8a" by clicking Start > Administrative Tools > Group Policy Management Configurator (GPMC)

6. In the tree view, expand Forest > Domains > corp.vlabs.local > Group Policy Objects

7. Select 'Group Policy Objects' open the context menu, (right-mouse-click on Group Policy Objects), select 'New'

8. Enter 'PasswordGPO' for the name and select 'OK'

9. Right click the newly created 'PasswordGPO' and select 'Edit...'

Current Version Date: 05/27/2011

10. In the Group Policy Management Editor tree view, expand Computer Configuration > Policies > Windows Settings > Security Settings > Account policies. Select 'Password Policy'.

11. Double-click 'Password must meet complexity requirements' and choose Enable. Choose 'OK'

12. Double-click 'Minimum Password Length' and enter 8. Choose 'OK'

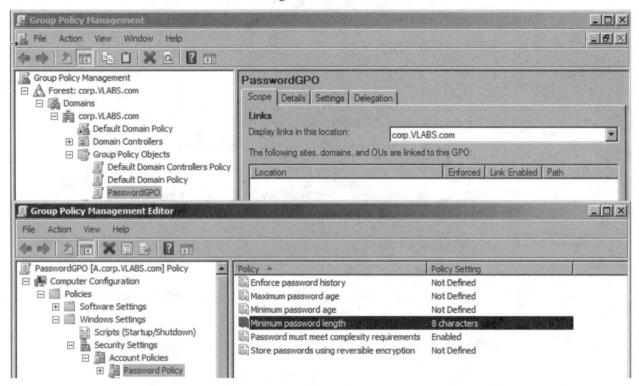

Figure 1 –Microsoft Windows Group Policy Management Editor

13. Next, you will disable the default Windows 2008 Password Complexity settings in the 'Default Domain Policy' via the Group Policy Manager.

14. From the Group Policy Management console Right Click the "Default Domain Policy" and click Edit

15. On the 'Default Domain Policy' drill down into Computer Configuration > Policies > Windows Settings > Security Settings > Account policies. Select 'Password Policy'

16. Double Click each of the default Windows 2008 Password Policy Settings and uncheck every box to leave them at a state of "Not Defined" and click OK.

17. Finally we will Right Click the Domain (corp.vlabs.local) at the top of the Tree View and click 'Link an Existing GPO...' and select our newly created 'PasswordGPO'.

18. Now the new 'PasswordGPO" Group Policy Object is linked and applied to our Domain instead of the Windows 2008 Default Password Policy settings.

Current Version Date: 05/27/2011

19. Close the Group Policy Management Editor.

Creating Users, Groups and Folders

20. Create and configure the following global domain users and groups using Active Directory Users and Computers (Start > Administrative Tools > Active Directory Users and Computers):

    a. Create the three following Global Security Groups:

        i. ShopFloor

        ii. HumanResources

        iii. Management

    b. Configure the user accounts with usernames, passwords and group memberships as follows:

        i. SFuser01 with a password of: ISSuser01 and member of the ShopFloor group

        ii. SFuser02 with a password of: ISSuser02 and member of the ShopFloor group

        iii. SFmanager with a password of: ISSmanager01 and member of both the ShopFloor and Management groups

        iv. HRuser01 with a password of: ISShumanresources01 and member of the HumanResources group

        v. HRuser02 with a password of: ISShumanresources02 and member of the HumanResources group

        vi. HRmanager with a password of: ISShumanresources03 and member of the HumanResources and Management groups

21. Logout of 'Target2k8a' and power up the 'Target2k8b' virtual machine.

22. Logon to 'Target2k8b' as Domain Administrator using the following username convention:

    Username: corp\administrator

    Password: ISS316Security

23. Create four new folders on any drive of the 'Target2k8b' virtual machine:

    a. \\ERPdocuments – Folder for shared ERP files

    b. \\ERPdocuments\HRfiles – Folder for shared Human Resources files

    c. \\ERPdocuments\SFfiles – Folder for shared Shop Floor files

    d. \\ERPdocuments\MGRfiles – Folder for shared Management files

24. Logout of 'Target2k8b' as administrator.

NOTE: To log into 'Target2k8b' with a newly created domain user account for the first time, the Domain Controller 'Target2k8a', **MUST** be running and responding to pings from 'Target2k8b'.

Current Version Date: 05/27/2011

25. Logon to 'Target2k8b' as SFuser01. Attempt to create a text file called: lab1_SFfile.txt in \\ERPdocuments\SFfiles

    Login: corp\SFUser01

    Password: ISSuser01

    Note: both the login and password are case-sensitive

26. Logout of 'Target2k8b' as SFuser01

27. Logon to 'Target2k8b' as HRuser01 and attempt to create a text file called: lab1_HRfile.txt in \\ERPdocuments\HRfiles

    Login: corp\HRUser01

    Password: ISShumanresources01

28. Determine what type of access controls are needed to allow the following actions:

    a. Prevent unauthorized users from logging onto another person's user account

    b. Allow Shop Floor users to read and write files in \\ERPdocuments\SFfiles

    c. Allow Human Resources users to read and write files in \\ERPdocuments\HRfiles

    d. SFManager users to read and write files in \\ERPdocuments\MGRfiles and \\ERPdocuments\SFfiles

    e. HRManager users to read and write files in \\ERPdocuments\MGRfiles and \\ERPdocuments\HRfiles

Deliverables

Upon completion of Lab #1 - Configure Active Directory and Implement Departmental and User Access, the students are required to provide the following deliverables:

1. Screenshot captures of the errors incurred when attempting to create files without proper permissions with a brief description of the attempted access and access control result

2. Lab #1 – Access Controls Criteria Worksheet

3. Lab #1 – Assessment Questions & Answers

Evaluation Criteria and Rubrics

The following are the evaluation criteria and rubrics for Lab #1 that the students must perform:

1. Was the student able to create Windows 2008 Standard Server R2 Active Directory system administration configurations for defined departmental workgroups and users? – [**20%**]

2. Was the student able to create Windows 2008 Standard Server R2 global domain departmental groups and user account definitions per defined access control requirements? – [**20%**]

3. Was the student able to configure Windows 2008 Standard Server R2 departmental group and user folders with unique access rights per the defined access control requirements? – [**20%**]

4. Was the student able to access a Windows 2008 Standard Server R2 as a user and encounter errors when attempting to create data files and write them to specific folders? – [**20%**]

5. Was the student able to create a list of new and modified access control parameters to implement stringent security access controls as per the defined requirements using Windows 2008 Standard Server R2? – [**20%**]

Current Version Date: 05/27/2011

Lab #1 – Access Controls Criteria Worksheet

Instructions

For the given access control requirements, specify what you need to implement to comply with the requirement.

Access Control Requirement	Access Control Implementation
Prevent unauthorized users from logging onto another person's user account with periodic password changes.	
Allow Shop Floor users to read and write files in C:\ ERPdocuments\SFfiles.	
Allow Human Resources users to read and write files in C:\ ERPdocuments\HRfiles.	
SFManager users to read and write files in C:\ ERPdocuments\MGRfiles and C:\ ERPdocuments\SFfiles.	
HRManager users to read and write files in C:\ ERPdocuments\MGRfiles and C:\ ERPdocuments\HRfiles.	

Lab #1 – Assessment Worksheet

Course Name & Number: _____

Student Name: _____

Instructor Name: _____

Lab Due Date: _____

Overview

This lab demonstrates how to configure Windows Server 2008 R2 Active Directory Departments, Users, and read/write folder and file access privileges. The students will use the Windows Configuration Applet and Group Policy Manager to create and test configurations and read/write of several files with specific access controls. They will use Group Policy Objects to restrict access to certain users and groups at the directory, folder, and file level. This configuration is critical to ensure the confidentiality and integrity of data. Role-based access controls at the directory, folder, and file level are implemented per defined access control requirements. The students will design and implement a layered security strategy using Windows Server 2008 R2 Active Directory.

Lab #1 Assessment Questions

1. Relate how Windows Server 2008 R2 Active Directory and the configuration of access controls achieve C-I-A for departmental LANs, departmental folders, and data.

2. Is it a good practice to include the account or user name in the password? Why or why not?

3. In order to enhance the strength of user passwords, what are some of the best practices to implement for user password definitions in order to maximize confidentiality?

4. Can a user defined in Active Directory access a shared drive if that user is not part of the domain?

5. Does Windows Server 2008 R2 require a user's login/password credentials prior to accessing shared drives?

Current Version Date: 05/27/2011

6. When looking at the Active Directory structure for Users and Computers, which group has the least amount of implied privileges?

7. When granting access to LAN systems for GUESTS (i.e., auditors, consultants, third-party individuals, etc.), what security controls do you recommend be implemented in order to maximize C-I-A of production systems and data?

8. When granting access for the Shop Floor group to the SFfiles within the SFfiles folder, what must be configured within Active Directory?

9. When granting access for the Human Resources group to access the HRfiles within the HRfiles folder, what must be configured within Active Directory?

10. Explain how C-I-A can be achieved down to the folder and data file access level for departments and its user's using Active Directory and Windows Server 2008 R2 access control configurations. Configuring unique access controls for different user types is an example of what kind of access controls?

Laboratory #2

Lab #2: Implement Access Control Lists to Secure Folders and Read/Write/Access to Files

Learning Objectives and Outcomes

Upon completing this equipment-based lab, students will be able to complete the following tasks:

- Align access control lists to control a user's ability to access Microsoft Windows resources

- Identify default access control list definitions for protected objects

- Design an access control list strategy to implement the principle of least privilege

- Implement access control lists as per the defined strategy

- Compare the differences between user-based access control lists with group based ACLs

Required Setup and Tools

The following are **required** for this equipment-based lab:

A) A classroom workstation with at least 4GB of RAM capable of supporting the removable hard drive with the VM server farm.

B) An Instructor workstation with at least 2 Gig RAM/4Gig RAM recommended that shall act as the instructor's demo lab workstation. The Instructor will display the workstation on the projector to demo the loading and configuring of the Target VMs using VMware Player.

C) Student Lab workstations will use their own VM server farm and classroom workstation. VMware Player will be used to run the Target VMs and perform the equipment-based steps.

NOTE: In this course only the virtual machines named 'Target2k8a' and 'Target2k8b' contained in the removable hard drive are required to perform equipment-based labs. The workstations with 4GB of RAM can support two Target VMs. Virtual machines can be Paused or Stopped when not in use in order to maximize performance. One VM at a time is recommended for a system with 2GB of RAM.

The following summarizes the setup, configuration, and equipment needed to perform Lab #2:

1. Standard classroom workstation and external hard drive with Virtual server farm

2. Virtual machines required for Lab #2:
   o 'Target2k8a' > same as > "Windows2k8a"
   o 'Target2k8b' > same as > "Windows2k8b"

Current Version Date: 05/27/2011

3. Target VM configurations are as follows:
   - Microsoft Windows 2008 Standard Server R2
   - Domain Name: corp.vlabs.local
   - Domain and Local Administrator access:
     - Username: administrator
     - Password: ISS316Security
   - 'Target2k8a' Roles installed: Active Directory Services and DNS

Equipment-Based Lab #2 – Student Steps

Part A - Configuring Access Controls Lists and Folder Permissions

1. Connect removable hard drive containing the Mock IT Server Farm to your workstation
2. Login to the classroom workstation using your login credentials
3. Power-up the "Target2k8b" virtual machine using VMware Player
4. Login to the "Target2k8b" as Domain Administrator:
5. Use each folder's properties dialog (Security tab) and the iCacls.exe command to review the current ACLs defined for the folders you created in Lab #1
6. To review the Security tab of each folder or file simply Right Click the folder or file and select Properties and click on the Security tab. All access controls and permissions are listed in this dialog box for every folder and file on a Windows system
7. To review the ACLs from the command line.exe you must run the proper icacls.exe commands from the Windows CMD shell (DOS prompt). Assuming you are evaluating ACLs on a folder located on the C:\ drive the command would look like the screenshot following

---

NOTE: The drive letter mapping where the folders and files are created is irrelevant. This command should work anywhere on the hard drive where the target folders and files are located.

Current Version Date: 05/27/2011

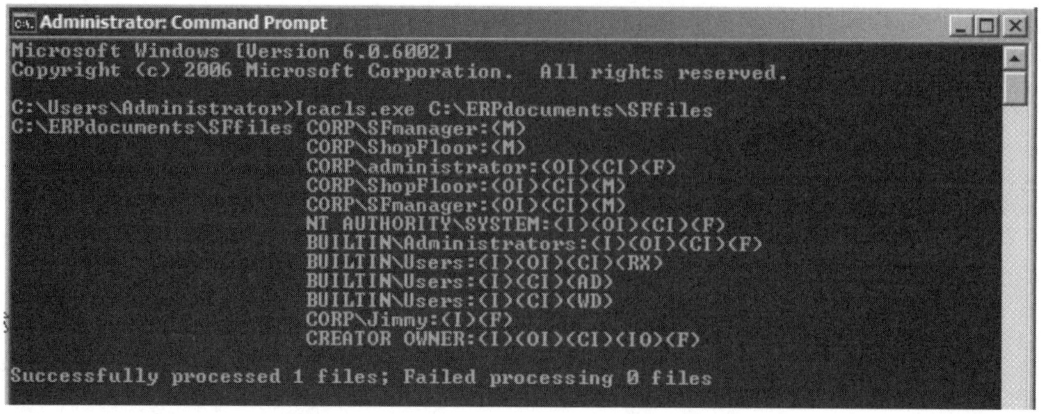

Figure 2 – Enable the icacls.exe Command to Review ACLs

8. Evaluate the default ACL security controls in terms of the following user access requirements:

   a. ShopFloor users should be able to create, delete, read and write files in \\ERPdocuments\SFfiles.

   b. HumanResources users should be able to create, delete, read and write files in \\ERPdocuments\HRfiles.

   c. ShopFloor Managers should be able to create, delete, read and write files in \\ERPdocuments\MFGfiles and \\ERPdocuments\SFfiles.

   d. Human Resources Managers should be able to create, delete, read and write files in \\ERPdocuments\MFGfiles and \\ERPdocuments\HRfiles.

9. Use icacls.exe to create new or modify existing ACLs to fulfill the access objectives from the previous step. For example the command line syntax used for icaclas.exe that will allow Modify, Read and Write permissions is as follows: icacls.exe [folder] /grant [user group]:(M,RX)

NOTE: If there is any doubt on the icacls.exe syntax or how to execute different commands with this utility simply type icacls.exe (the command only with no arguments) and hit enter in the Windows command line. This will print to screen the help file and the entire syntax options with which any feature of the icalcs.exe utility can be executed.

Part B - Verifying Access Controls and Permissions

10. Logout of 'Target2k8b' as Domain Administrator

11. Login to 'Target2k8b' as SFuser01: corp\sfuser01

Current Version Date: 05/27/2011

12. Use notepad to create a new text file, lab1_SFfile.txt, in \\ERPdocuments\SFfiles. You should now be able to do this successfully if the proper permissions have been granted to this user during the icacls.exe steps

13. Attempt to create a new text file, lab1_HRfile.txt, in \\ERPdocuments\HRfiles. You should be denied access and not able to create this file here

14. Logout of "Target2k8b" and log back in as SFuser02: corp\sfuser02

15. Open \\ERPdocuments\SFfiles\lab1_SFfile.txt; make a change to the file, then save it. Your access controls should allow both SFuser01 and SFuser02 to create, read, and write files in \\ERPdocuments\SFfiles. The file changes should have been successful

16. Logout of "Target2k8b" and log back in as HRuser01: corp\hruser01
    Use notepad to create a new text file, lab2_HRfile.txt, in \\ERPdocuments\HRfiles

17. Attempt to create a new text file, lab2_SFfile.txt, in \\ERPdocuments\SFfiles. This access should be denied, and you should not be able to create this file in this folder

18. Logout of "Target2k8b" and log back in as HRuser01: corp\hruser02

19. Open \\ERPdocuments\HRfiles\lab2_HRfile.txt; make a change to the file, then save it. Your access controls should allow both HRuser01 and HRuser02 to create, read, and write files in \\ERPdocuments\HRfiles. You should be successful doing this edit and change to this file in this folder

20. Logout of "Target2k8b" and log back in as SFmanager: corp\sfmanager

21. Verify that you can read and write files in \\ERPdocuments\SFfiles and \\ERPdocuments\MGRfile, but not in \\ERPdocuments\HRfiles

22. Document what access controls and rights SFmanager has in these folders

23. Logout of "Target2k8b" and log back in as HRmanager: corp\hrmanager

24. Verify that you can read and write files in \\ERPdocuments\HRfiles and \\ERPdocuments\MGRfiles, but not \\ERPdocuments\SFfiles

25. Document what access controls and rights HRmanager has in these folders

Deliverables

Upon completion of this lab, students are required to provide the following deliverables:

1. Lab #2 – Access Control Lists definitions for each of the four folders created in Lab #1

2. Lab #2 – Access Control Lists Worksheet

3. Lab #2 – Assessment Questions & Answers

Evaluation Criteria and Rubrics

The following are the evaluation criteria and rubrics for Lab #2 that the students must perform:

1. Was the student able to align access control lists to control a user's ability to access Microsoft Windows resources? – **[20%]**

2. Was the student able to identify default access control list definitions for protected objects? – **[20%]**

3. Was the student able to design an access control list strategy to implement the principle of least privilege? – **[20%]**

4. Was the student able to implement access control lists as per the defined strategy? – **[20%]**

5. Was the student able to compare the differences between user based access control lists with group based ACLs? – **[20%]**

Lab #2 – Access Control Lists Worksheet

Instructions

For each access control requirements, specify what you recommend for implementation of the access control requirement.

Access Control Requirements	Access Control Implementation
Prevent unauthorized users from logging onto another person's user account.	
Allow Shop Floor users to read and write files in C:\ ERPdocuments\SFfiles.	
Allow Human Resources users to read and write files in C:\ ERPdocuments\HRfiles.	
SFManager users to read and write files in C:\ ERPdocuments\MGRfiles and C:\ ERPdocuments\SFfiles.	
HRManager users to read and write files in C:\ ERPdocuments\MGRfiles and C:\ ERPdocuments\HRfiles.	

Current Version Date: 05/27/2011

Lab #2 – Assessment Worksheet

Course Name & Number: _____

Student Name: _____

Instructor Name: _____

Lab Due Date: _____

Overview

This lab demonstrates how to use icalcs.exe in a Microsoft Windows environment to evaluate and list all of the access control lists associated with a given object in Windows. iCalcs.exe also allows users to modify a file's access control lists directly from the DOS command prompt using character line interface commands. For administrators editing or evaluating access control lists on many files and directories the iCalcs.exe tool is indispensible allowing immediate, scriptable capabilities for large scale enterprise-wide access control list modifications and analysis.

Lab #2 Assessment Questions

1. What is the Principle of Least Privilege?

2. What does DACL stands for and what does it mean?

3. Why would you add permissions to a group instead of the individual?

4. Why would you allow shared access to groups instead of to everyone?

5. List at least 3 different types of access control permissions you can enable for a file.

6. Which access control permissions allow you to delete files and/or folders?

7. What is the lowest level permission needed in order to view the contents of a folder?

Current Version Date: 05/27/2011

8. If you don't remember the syntax when using iCacls.exe what command do you type in to see the options?

9. What other tool could you use to modify the privileges of the files or folders of a shared drive?

10. During the lab exercise were you able to create, modify or delete a text file on Server B as SFmanager or HRmanager? Explain.

Laboratory #3

Lab #3: Enable Encryption on a Microsoft Server to Ensure Confidentiality

Learning Objectives and Outcomes

Upon completing this equipment-based lab, students will be able to complete the following tasks:

- Relate how a data classification standard will dictate whether or not certain folders and files need encryption while residing on hard drives within the Workstation Domain
- Identify requirements for Microsoft BitLocker and EFS to maximize confidentiality by encrypting the hard disk, folders and files
- Implement Microsoft's Encrypting File System (EFS) on a Windows Server 2008 R2
- Implement Microsoft's BitLocker Drive Encryption on a Windows Server 2008 R2
- Verify privacy data is encrypted and cannot be accessed on EFS enabled folders and data files

Required Setup and Tools

The following are **required** for this equipment-based lab:

A) A classroom workstation with at least 4GB of RAM capable of supporting the removable hard drive with the VM server farm.

B) An Instructor workstation with at least 2 Gig RAM/4Gig RAM recommended that shall act as the instructor's demo lab workstation. The Instructor will display the workstation on the projector to demo the loading and configuring of the Target VMs using VMware Player.

C) Student Lab workstations will use their own VM server farm and classroom workstation. VMware Player will be used to run the Target VMs and perform the equipment-based steps.

NOTE: 'TargetWindows02' Release 2 VM is required for this lab. Be sure to download Release 2 and add to your Mock IT Infrastructure VM server farm. This 'TargetWindows02' Release 2 VM is for use only with the BitLocker portion of this lab.

Current Version Date: 05/27/2011

NOTE: The virtual machines named 'Target2k8a' and 'Target2k8b' contained in the removable hard drive are required to perform this and every other equipment-based lab. The workstations with 4GB of RAM can support two Target VMs. One VM at a time is recommended for a system with 2GB of RAM.

The following summarizes the setup, configuration, and equipment needed to perform Lab #3:

Microsoft Encrypting File System (EFS) – (from www.microsoft.com – security tech center)

"One solution to help reduce the potential for stolen data is to encrypt sensitive files by using Encrypting File System (EFS) to increase the security of your data. Encryption is the application of a mathematical algorithm to make data unreadable except to those users who have the required key. EFS is a Microsoft technology that lets you encrypt data on your computer, and control who can decrypt, or recover, the data. When files are encrypted, user data cannot be read even if an attacker has physical access to the computer's data storage. To use EFS, all users must have Encrypting File System certificates-digital documents that allow their holders to encrypt and decrypt data using EFS. EFS users must also have NTFS permission to modify the files.

To enable another authorized person to read your encrypted data, you can give them your private key, or you can make them a data recovery agent. A data recovery agent can decrypt all EFS-encrypted files in the domain or organizational unit in his or her scope. This document provides step-by-step instructions for the main EFS-related tasks in a small-to-medium business, and also lists several important best practices for using EFS."

Microsoft Bitlocker – (from www.microsoft.com – security tech center)

BitLocker Drive Encryption is a data protection feature available Windows Server 2008 R2 and in some editions of Windows 7. Having BitLocker integrated with the operating system addresses the threats of data theft or exposure from lost, stolen, or inappropriately decommissioned computers.

The data on a lost or stolen computer is vulnerable to unauthorized access, either by running a software-attack tool against it or by transferring the computer's hard disk to a different computer. BitLocker helps mitigate unauthorized data access by enhancing file and system protections. It also helps render data inaccessible when BitLocker-protected computers are decommissioned or recycled.

Current Version Date: 05/27/2011

BitLocker provides the most protection when used with a Trusted Platform Module (TPM) version 1.2. The TPM is a hardware component installed in many newer computers by the computer manufacturers. It works with BitLocker to help protect user data and to ensure that a computer has not been tampered with while the system was offline.

On computers that do not have a TPM version 1.2, you can still use BitLocker to encrypt the Windows operating system drive. However, this implementation will require the user to insert a USB startup key to start the computer or resume from hibernation, and it does not provide the pre-startup system integrity verification offered by BitLocker with a TPM.

In addition to the TPM, BitLocker offers the option to lock the normal startup process until the user supplies a personal identification number (PIN) or inserts a removable device, such as a USB flash drive, that contains a startup key. These additional security measures provide multifactor authentication and assurance that the computer will not start or resume from hibernation until the correct PIN or startup key is entered.

The following summarizes the setup, configuration, and equipment needed to perform Lab #3:

1. Standard classroom workstation and the Virtual Server Farm
2. Windows 2008 STD Server R2 virtual machines required for Lab #3 are as follows:
   - 'Target2k8a': A Domain Controller for a new Forest used throughout this course
     - Domain Name: corp.vlabs.local
     - Role: Domain Controller with Active Directory and DNS Services installed
     - Domain Administrator access for 'Target2k8a' and 'Target2k8b' is as follows:
       - Username: corp\administrator
       - Password: ISS316Security
   - 'Target2k8b': A domain member server used for the **EFS** portion of this lab **ONLY**
   - 'TargetWindows02': A stand-alone server used for the **BitLocker** portion of this lab **ONLY**
     - Local Administrator access for 'TargetWindows02' is as follows:
       - Username: administrator
       - Password: ISS316Security

Current Version Date: 05/27/2011

Equipment-Based Lab #3 – Student Steps

For equipment-based Lab #3, students are required to perform the following steps:

1. Connect your removable hard drive containing the VM Server Farm to your classroom workstation.
2. Login to the classroom workstation using your login credentials.
3. Power-up the "Target2k8b" virtual machine using VMware Player.

Microsoft Encrypting File System (EFS)

"One solution to help reduce the potential for stolen data is to encrypt sensitive files by using Encrypting File System (EFS) to increase the security of your data. Encryption is the application of a mathematical algorithm to make data unreadable except to those users who have the required key. EFS is a Microsoft technology that lets you encrypt data on your computer, and control who can decrypt, or recover, the data. When files are encrypted, user data cannot be read even if an attacker has physical access to the computer's data storage. To use EFS, all users must have Encrypting File System certificates-digital documents that allow their holders to encrypt and decrypt data using EFS. EFS users must also have NTFS permission to modify the files. To enable another authorized person to read your encrypted data, you can give them your private key, or you can make them a data recovery agent. A data recovery agent can decrypt all EFS-encrypted files in the domain or organizational unit in his or her scope. This document provides step-by-step instructions for the main EFS-related tasks in a small-to-medium business, and also lists several important best practices for using EFS."

For this part of the lab, you will enable EFS on a specific user's document folder and files. A Data Classification Standard is dictating that you encrypt a folder with data files containing customer privacy data. Because of this policy, you must enable EFS encryption on a designated system folder and its data files as a security control for storage of data containing privacy data elements. Since EFS uses keys based on the user's password, this encryption method is for individual user's folders and files and not shared folders and documents. Follow these instructions for enabling EFS on a specific user folder and files:

Enable Microsoft EFS on Files and Folders

4. Login to "Target2k8b" as a SFuser01
   - Username: corp\sfuser01
   - Password: ISSuser01

Current Version Date: 05/27/2011

5. Open Windows Explorer and navigate to SFuser01's Documents folder. When logged in as SFuser01 then the Documents folder should be found here: C:\Users\SFuser01\Documents

6. Create a text file called: lab3_SFfile.txt

7. Open the text file and type in: "**This is a test to verify encryption functionality**", Save and Close the text file

8. To encrypt the Documents folder, go up one directory to the user's home directory, right click the Documents folder and select 'Properties'

9. From the Document Properties Dialog, choose the 'Advanced' button

10. In the "Advanced Attributes" menu, select the 'Encrypt contents to secure data' by checking the box, choose 'OK', then choose 'OK' again to close the properties menu dialog

11. Next verify that the Documents folder and its contents have been encrypted by Right Clicking the Documents Folder again and click Properties > Advanced Attributes

12. Verify that the "Encrypt..." attribute is checked in the Documents folder properties

13. Logout of 'Target2k8b" as SFuser01

14. Login to 'Target2k8b' as Domain Administrator

15. Browse to C:\Users\SFuser01\Documents and attempt to access the folder

16. Now try to open and read the file created by SFuser01

Microsoft BitLocker

BitLocker Drive Encryption is a data protection feature available Windows Server 2008 R2 and in some editions of Windows 7. Having BitLocker integrated with the operating system addresses the threats of data theft or exposure from lost, stolen, or inappropriately decommissioned computers.

The data on a lost or stolen computer is vulnerable to unauthorized access, either by running a software-attack tool against it or by transferring the computer's hard disk to a different computer. BitLocker helps mitigate unauthorized data access by enhancing file and system protections. It also helps render data inaccessible when BitLocker-protected computers are decommissioned or recycled.

BitLocker provides the most protection when used with a Trusted Platform Module (TPM) version 1.2. The TPM is a hardware component installed in many newer computers by the computer manufacturers. It works with BitLocker to help protect user data and to ensure that a computer has not been tampered with while the system was offline. On computers that do not have a TPM version 1.2, you can still use BitLocker to encrypt the Windows operating system drive. However, this implementation will require the

Current Version Date: 05/27/2011

user to insert a USB startup key to start the computer or resume from hibernation, and it does not provide the pre-startup system integrity verification offered by BitLocker with a TPM. In addition to the TPM, BitLocker offers the option to lock the normal startup process until the user supplies a personal identification number (PIN) or inserts a removable device, such as a USB flash drive, that contains a startup key. These additional security measures provide multifactor authentication and assurance that the computer will not start or resume from hibernation until the correct PIN or startup key is entered.

For this part of the lab, you will enable BitLocker on a Microsoft 2008 Server R2. For servers in a shared or potentially non-secure environment, such as a branch office location, BitLocker can be used to encrypt the operating system drive and additional data drives on the same server. By default, BitLocker is not installed with Windows Server 2008 R2. Add BitLocker from the Windows Server 2008 R2 Server Manager page. You must restart after installing BitLocker on a server. Using WMI, you can enable BitLocker remotely. BitLocker is supported on Extensible Firmware Interface (EFI) servers that use a 64-bit processor architecture. After the drive has been encrypted and protected with BitLocker, local and domain administrators can use the Manage BitLocker page in the BitLocker Drive Encryption item in Control Panel to change the password to unlock the drive, remove the password from the drive, add a smart card to unlock the drive, save or print the recovery key again, automatically unlock the drive, duplicate keys, and reset the PIN. BitLocker uses the computer's TPM chip to store encryption keys and does not rely on individual user credentials.

Enable Microsoft BitLocker Drive Encryption

17. Log into 'TargetWindows02' as Local Administrator:
    - Username: administrator
    - Password: ISS316Security
18. First we will verify that the use of a TPM module which is typically required for BitLocker is disabled in the Local Security Policy

NOTE: Because this is a Virtual Machine and not a Physical Machine with access to a TPM in the System BIOS you will need a USB stick/hard drive (use your student USB hard drive) to store the complete BitLocker encryption process.

19. Go to START. Type in mmc and press <Enter>.
20. In the drop-down list under the File tab, select Add/Remove Snap-in…

21. Add the Group Policy Object snap-in and select Local.

22. Edit the Local Security Policy by browsing to Computer Configuration > Administrative Templates > Windows Components > BitLocker Drive Encryption.

23. Double click on Control Panel Setup: Advanced Startup Options > Set to Enabled if it isn't already and make sure that Allow BitLocker without a compatible TPM is checked.

24. Click Apply and OK.

25. Click Start > Server Manager.

26. Select 'Features' in the tree view to open the Features detail window.

27. Select 'Add Features'.

28. Check the box next to 'Bitlocker Drive Encryption' then select 'Next'.

29. Follow the wizard instructions for installing the Bitlocker feature on the server.

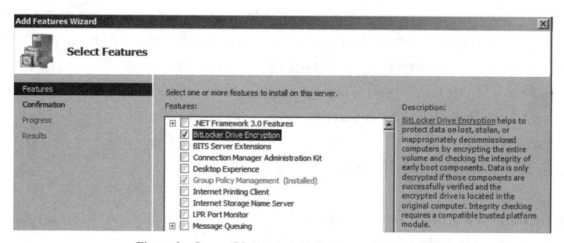

Figure 3 – Server Manager Add Features: BitLocker

30. Click Start > Control Panel > BitLocker Drive Encryption.

31. Select 'Turn on BitLocker' for the desired drive (Typically only volume C:\ is encrypted unless you have added additional virtual disks to the provided VM).

32. Select the Continue with BitLocker Drive Encryption.

33. Because there is no TPM available to store the security key on the system you will need to save the BitLocker security key to an external USB key.

34. Select Require Startup USB key at every startup the click 'Next'. .

35. Name the file "Securing Windows Lab #3 Key" for the recovery key then select 'Save'.

36. Choose 'Next' then 'Start Encrypting' to encrypt the selected drive.

37. Upon completion, verify that the operating system drive has been encrypted by attempting to start the virtual machine **WITHOUT** the recovery key available.

Deliverables

Upon completion of this lab, students are required to provide the following deliverables:

1. Lab #3 – Screen Capture of EFS Folder Encryption Screen – submit a screen capture of the folder that you enabled EFS and the verify encryption of the data files

2. Lab #3 – Screen Capture of Bitlocker Shared Drive Encryption – submit a screen capture of the Volume (D:) drive that you Bitlocked and verify encryption of the entire shared drive

3. Lab #3 – Assessment Questions & Answers

Evaluation Criteria and Rubrics

The following are the evaluation criteria and rubrics for Lab #3 that the students must perform:

1. Was the student able to relate how a data classification standard will dictate whether or not certain folders and files need encryption while residing on hard drives within the Workstation Domain? – [**20%**]

2. Was the student able to identify requirements for Microsoft Bitlocker and EFS to maximize confidentiality by encrypting folders and files? – [**20%**]

3. Was the student able to implement Microsoft's Bitlocker on a shared drive using Windows Server 2008 R2? – [**20%**]

4. Was the student able to implement Microsoft's Encrypting File System (EFS) on user data folder using Windows Server 2008 R2? – [**20%**]

5. Was the student able to verify privacy data is encrypted and cannot be accessed on EFS enabled or Bitlocked folders, drives, and data files? – [**20%**]

Current Version Date: 05/27/2011

Lab #3 – Assessment Worksheet

Course Name & Number: _____

Student Name: _____

Instructor Name: _____

Lab Due Date: _____

Overview

This equipment-based lab presented solutions for maximizing confidentiality for data residing either within a user's folder or on a shared volume drive. The students will enable Microsoft's Encryption File System (EFS) on a user folder to encrypt its contents. In addition, Microsoft Bitlocker will be enabled on a shared volume drive to encrypt its contents on a shared LAN disk drive. They must report how a Data Classification Standard impacts the Workstation Domain and determines the need to encrypt user folders and the LAN Domain requiring encryption of shared drives on LAN servers.

Lab #3 - Assessment Questions

1. Within a Microsoft Windows 2008 Server R2 environment, who has access rights to the EFS features and functions in the server?

2. There are three modes of access control that Bitlocker can enable on drives. List these three modes.

3. What feature and function can you enable to mitigate the risk caused by USB thumb drives moving confidential data to/from a USB hard drive?

4. What are some best practices you can implement when encrypting BitLocker drives and the use of Bitlocker recovery passwords?

5. What encryption algorithm is supported BitLocker?

6. What is the Trusted Platform Module (TPM) within Bitlocker and how does this verify the integrity of the Workstation Domain and laptops boot process?

7. How do you add additional user's to have access rights to your EFS encrypted folders and data files?

Current Version Date: 05/27/2011

8. How do you create a backup of your certificate?

9. What are the main differences between EFS and BitLocker?

10. A Data Classification Standard has defined customer privacy data as requiring encryption while residing in hard drives or disk drives within the Workstation Domain and LAN Domain. Users that have access to and that store customer privacy data on their personal user data folders must be encrypted. Customer privacy data residing on shared disk drives on LANs must also be encrypted while residing on shared drives. Describe your solution for meeting this policy requirement.

Current Version Date: 05/27/2011

Laboratory #4

Lab #4: Identify, Remove, and Verify Malware and Malicious Software on a Microsoft Workstation

Learning Objectives and Outcomes

Upon completing this equipment-based lab, students will be able to complete the following tasks:

- Identify malware and malicious software infected on a Microsoft Workstation
- Remove malware and malicious software from an infected Microsoft Workstation
- Verify that the infected Microsoft Workstation has been cleared of malware and malicious software
- Identify, scan, and remove malicious spyware using Microsoft Windows Defender
- Recommend best practices for proactive malware, spyware, and malicious software prevention within the Workstation Domain

Required Setup and Tools

The following are **required** for this equipment-based lab:

A) A classroom workstation with at least 4GB of RAM capable of supporting the removable hard drive with the VM server farm.

B) An Instructor workstation with at least 2 Gig RAM/4Gig RAM recommended that shall act as the instructor's demo lab workstation. The Instructor will display the workstation on the projector to demo the loading and configuring of the Target VMs using VMware Player.

C) Student Lab workstations will use their own VM server farm and classroom workstation. VMware Player will be used to run the Target VMs and perform the equipment-based steps.

NOTE: Workstations with 4GB of RAM can support two Target VMs. Virtual machines can be Paused or Stopped when not in use in order to maximize performance. No more than one VM at a time is recommended for a system with 2GB of RAM.

The following summarizes the setup, configuration, and equipment needed to perform Lab #4:

1. Standard classroom workstation and the Virtual Server Farm
2. Internet Access for the classroom workstation is **required** to properly complete this lab

Current Version Date: 05/27/2011

NOTE: Do **NOT** disconnect the classroom from the Internet for this lab!

3. Virtual machines required for Lab #4 are as follows:

   o 'Target2k8a': A Domain Controller for a new Forest used throughout this course

      ▪ Microsoft Windows Defender, an integrated Windows malware detection tool

      ▪ Domain Name: corp.vlabs.local

      ▪ Role: Domain Controller with Active Directory and DNS Services installed

      ▪ Domain Administrator access is as follows:

         o Username: corp\administrator

         o Password: ISS316Security

   o 'WindowsVulnerable01': A vulnerable, and possibly infected, Windows XP workstation

      ▪ Avast Antivirus free version (http://www.avast.com) **must be downloaded and installed** (Almost any similar free antivirus tool can also be used based on instructor preference)

      ▪ Local Administrator access is as follows:

         o Username: administrator

         o Password: ISS316Security

Equipment-Based Lab #4 – Student Steps

For equipment-based Lab #4, students are required to perform the following steps:

1. Connect your removable hard drive containing the VM Server Farm to your classroom workstation.

2. Login to the classroom workstation using your login credentials.

NOTE: For proper completion of this lab your ITT classroom workstation will require a **LIVE** Internet connection. Do **NOT** disconnect the student workstations from the classroom network and Internet connection.

Running Anti-virus and Anti-malware Software on a Windows Workstation

3. Power-up the "WindowsVulnerable01" virtual machine and verify that you have Internet access.

4. From here you can download a FREE version of Avast's Antivirus, Anti-Spyware, Anti-Malicious Software application from the "WindowsVulnerable01" virtual machine to the Desktop: http://download.cnet.com/Avast-Free-Antivirus/3000-2239_4-10019223.html

5. Click and download the Avast "setup_av_free.exe" install program to the Desktop of the "WindowsVulnerable01" VM workstation

Current Version Date: 05/27/2011

6. Run the "setup_av_free.exe" install program and run the Avast Antivirus installation

7. Launch the Avast Antivirus application: Start > Programs > avast! Free Antivirus > avast! Free Antivirus

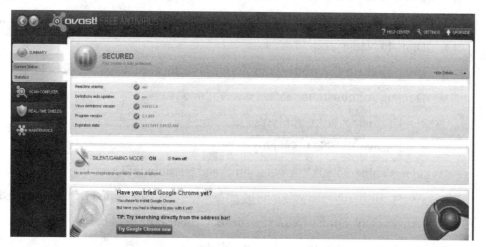

Figure 4 – Avast Antivirus Summary Screen

8. Click the "Maintenance" button and click "Update engine and virus definitions"

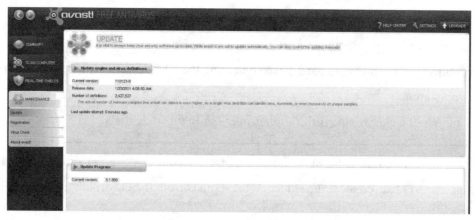

Figure 5 – Download Updated Virus Definitions

9. Select the "Scan Computer" button and select "Start" to perform the "Full Scan" on your "WindowsVulnerable01" virtual machine.

10. Document or perform a screen capture at the end of your "Full Scan" and submit that part of your Lab #4 deliverables.

11. For each malware instance Avast identifies, document the program Avast reports and take action to eradicate it. Document the action taken, if any.

Current Version Date: 05/27/2011

12. Review the other Avast anti-spyware, anti-malicious software applications and tools provided by Avast in the "Real-Time Shields" menu.

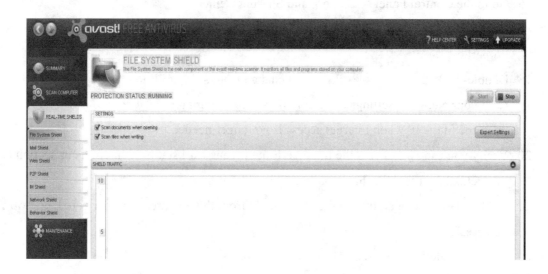

Figure 6 – Real-Time Shields – Anti Malicious Software Protection

Running Anti-virus and Anti-malware Software on a Windows 2008 Server

13. Shutdown the "WindowsVulnerable01" virtual machine and start up "Target2k8a".

NOTE: For 'Target2k8a' to be able to "Update" the Windows Defender application signatures, just like with 'WindowsVulnerable01' your classroom workstation and virtual machine **MUST** have access to the Internet. To do this you must change the Network Settings of 'Target2k8a' and possibly for your VMware Player as described below.

14. In VMware Player verify that the Network Settings for "Target2k8a" is set to NAT – **NOT** Bridged or Host-only by checking the Virtual Machines Settings for "Target2k8a"

NOTE: 'Target2k8a' is a Domain Controller for a new Forest in use ONLY in this course. Although it will work, this VM should **NOT** be configured in "Bridged" mode and put onto the LAN. Instead because it needs Internet access; the Network Settings should be configured to "NAT". "Host-only" will not work because it air-gaps the VM from all network and Internet access.

15. Login to the "Target2k8a" using the following credentials:

Current Version Date: 05/27/2011

- Username: corp\administrator
- Password: ISS316Security

16. Go to the Control Panel > Network and Sharing Center

17. Click "Manage Network Connections", right click your Local Area Connection and go to Properties.

18. Double-click "Internet TCP/IP v4" and change from a Static IP to a Dynamic IP.

19. Note your Network Settings and Static IP before changing to DHCP as you will need to reapply the same Static IP when Internet access is no longer needed.

20. Verify you can now access the Internet through your workstation's Internet connection and your 'Target2k8a' virtual machine configured in NAT mode.

21. Click "Start" and open the "Server Manager", from the Features Summary click on "Add Features".

22. From the Add Features Wizard select "Desktop Experience" and click on "Next".

23. Now confirm the selection by clicking on "Install". The installation will take some time.

24. For the new feature (Windows Defender) to take effect you must restart the server. Click on "Close" and you will be prompted to restart the server.

25. After the server starts allow for some time to complete the installation and configuration. If everything is OK you should see a message confirming the installation. Then click on "Close"

26. To start Windows Defender go to Start > All Programs > Windows Defender

27. Select and run the "Windows Defender" application.

28. Choose the "Update" button to get the latest spyware definitions.

29. Select the arrow next to the 'Scan' button and select "Quick Scan" to start the Windows Defender Quick Scan.

Current Version Date: 05/27/2011

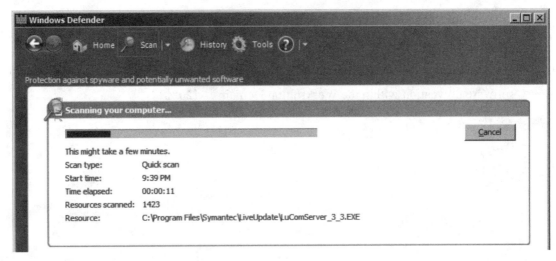

Figure 7 – Windows Defender – Quick Scan

30. For each spyware instance Windows Defender identifies, document the program Windows Defender reports and take action to eradicate it. Document the action taken, if any.

Deliverables

Upon completion of this lab, students are required to provide the following deliverables:

1. Lab #4 – Submit a screen shot of your Avira "Full Scan" results (Print Screen, Paste in Microsoft Paint, Copy and Paste) in a Microsoft Word document. Write a paragraph summarizing the findings and results of your scan.

2. Lab #4 – Submit a screen shot of your Windows 2008 Server R2 Windows Defender "Quick Scan" results in a Microsoft Word document. Write a paragraph summarizing the findings and results of your scan.

3. Lab #4 - Assessment Questions & Answers

Evaluation Criteria and Rubrics

The following are the evaluation criteria and rubrics for Lab #4 that the students must demonstrate:

1. Was the student able to identify malware and malicious software that infected a Microsoft Workstation? – [**20%**]

2. Was the student able to remove malware and malicious software from an infected Microsoft Workstation? – [**20%**]

3. Was the student able to verify that the infected Microsoft Workstation has been cleared of malware and malicious software? – [**20%**]

Current Version Date: 05/27/2011

4. Was the student able to identify, scan, and remove malicious spyware using Microsoft Windows Defender? – [**20%**]

5. Was the student able to recommend best practices for proactive malware, spyware, and malicious software prevention within the Workstation Domain? – [**20%**]

Current Version Date: 05/27/2011

Lab #4 – Assessment Worksheet

Course Name & Number: _____

Student Name: _____

Instructor Name: _____

Lab Due Date: _____

Overview

In order to combat the risks and threats commonly found within the Workstation Domain, workstations must be properly equipped with up-to-date anti-virus, anti-spyware, and anti-malicious software applications and tools. This is especially true for Microsoft Windows environments that dominate in the world of personal and corporate users. Security applications such as anti-virus, anti-malware, and anti-malicious software are critical to ensure the C-I-A of the Workstation Domain and the contents on that workstation.

Lab #4 - Assessment Questions

1. What is the one thing that a virus, a worm, spyware, and malicious code have in common? What are the differences among these four threats: a virus, a worm, spyware, and a malicious code?

2. How often should you update your anti-virus protection?

3. Why is it a best practice to have and to carry an antivirus boot-up disc or CD?

4. What other anti-malicious software and anti-malicious code applications are included with Avira under the Real-Time Shields application? What risk and threats do these help mitigate?

5. In a corporate environment, should new AV definitions be installed as soon as they are available?

6. Is the quick scan good enough to maintain the system protected?

Current Version Date: 05/27/2011

7. Besides the ones mentioned above, what other best practices are there for the Workstation Domain that can mitigate the risks and threats caused by malicious code?

8. If you have an up-to-date AV, do you still need a Malware detection program like Windows Defender?

9. What are some of the most common symptoms of malware?

10. What are examples of harmful spyware applications? What risk or threat do they pose to the Workstation Domain?

Laboratory #5

Lab #5: Configure Access Rights to Folder & Files Using Microsoft GPO Manager & Enable Microsoft BSA to Define a Security Baseline Definition

Learning Objectives and Outcomes

Upon completing this equipment-based lab, students will be able to complete the following tasks:

- Define and deploy Active Directory Group Policy Objects (GPO)

- Edit and deploy Security Policies across an Active Directory Domain using Group Policy Management Console (GPMC)

- Use Microsoft Baseline Security Analyzer (MBSA) to security baseline a Windows 2008 Server and a Windows XP Professional Workstation

- Analyze the output of the MBSA scan results from both Windows 2008 and Windows XP to identify vulnerabilities including remediation steps for identified vulnerabilities

Required Setup and Tools

The following are **required** for this equipment-based lab:

A) A classroom workstation with at least 4GB of RAM capable of supporting the removable hard drive with the VM server farm.

B) An Instructor workstation with at least 2 Gig RAM/4Gig RAM recommended that shall act as the instructor's demo lab workstation. The Instructor will display the workstation on the projector to demo the loading and configuring of the Target VMs using VMware Player.

C) Student Lab workstations will use their own VM server farm and classroom workstation. VMware Player will be used to run the Target VMs and perform the equipment-based steps.

NOTE: To properly complete the **MBSA** portion of this equipment-based lab **ANY** Windows 2008 Server and Windows XP virtual machine can be used. In these steps 'TargetWindows02' and either the 'Student' or 'Instructor' Windows XP virtual machines are used. The workstations with 4GB of RAM can run two Target VMs at once. One VM at a time is recommended for a system with 2GB of RAM.

The following summarizes the setup, configuration, and equipment needed to perform Lab #5:

1. Standard classroom workstation and the Virtual Server Farm

Current Version Date: 05/27/2011

2. The most recent version of Microsoft Baseline Security Analyzer (MBSA) must be downloaded

3. Virtual machines required for Lab #5 are as follows:

    a. "Target2k8a": A Domain Controller for a new Forest used throughout this course

        i. Domain Name: corp.vlabs.local

        ii. Role: Domain Controller with Active Directory and DNS Services installed

        iii. Domain Administrator access is as follows:

            o Username: corp\administrator

            o Password: ISS316Security

    b. "TargetWindows02" (or any of the provided Windows 2008 Server virtual machines): A stand-alone server used for the **BitLocker** portion of this lab **ONLY**

        i. MBSA: http://www.microsoft.com/downloads/en/details.aspx?FamilyID=b1e76bbe-71df-41e8-8b52-c871d012ba78 **must be downloaded and installed** (either from the classroom workstation BEFORE the lab or directly from the VM during the lab)

        ii. Local Administrator access for 'TargetWindows02' is as follows:

            o Username: administrator

            o Password: ISS316Security

    c. "Student" or "Instructor" (or any of the provided Windows XP Workstation virtual machines): A Windows XP workstation

        i. MBSA: http://www.microsoft.com/downloads/en/details.aspx?FamilyID=b1e76bbe-71df-41e8-8b52-c871d012ba78 **must be downloaded and installed** (either from the classroom workstation BEFORE the lab or directly from the VM during the lab)

        ii. Local Administrator access is as follows:

            o Username: administrator

            o Password: ISS316Security

Equipment-Based Lab #5 – Student Steps

For equipment-based Lab #5, students are required to perform the following steps:

1. Connect your external hard drive containing the VM Server Farm to your classroom workstation.

2. Login to the classroom workstation using your login credentials.

Current Version Date: 05/27/2011

3. Download Microsoft's Baseline Security Analyzer tools to the your classroom workstation: http://www.microsoft.com/downloads/en/details.aspx?displaylang=en&FamilyID=02be8aee-a3b6-4d94-b1c9-4b1989e0900c

Using Microsoft GPO Manager to Analyze and Deploy Group Policy Objects

4. Logon to 'Target2k8a' as Domain Administrator

   - Username: corp\administrator

   - Password: ISS316Security

5. Launch GPMC: Start > Administrative Tools > Group Policy Management

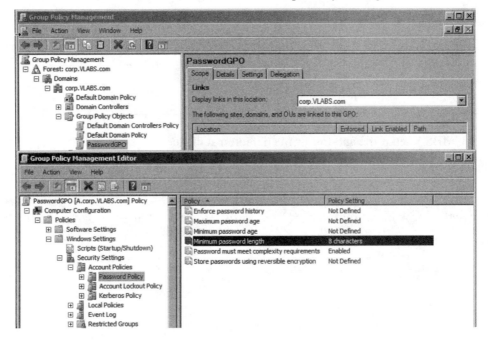

Figure 8 – Microsoft Windows Group Policy Management Editor

6. In the tree view, expand Forest > Domains > corp.vlabs.local > Group Policy Objects

7. Select "Group Policy Objects" right click the "Default Domain Policy" and select "Edit..."

8. In the Group Policy Management Editor treeview, expand Computer Configuration > Policies > Windows Settings > Security Settings

9. Review the settings under Account Policies, Local Policies, and Event Log sections.

10. Modify one of the policy settings of your choice and save the changes.

11. Close the GPO Editor and return to the GPMC.

12. Right click the "Default Domain Policy" and choose "Save Report".

Current Version Date: 05/27/2011

13. Enter the desired filename and folder to save the "Default Domain Policy" report

14. Attempt to verify if the setting that you have modified is in effect.

15. Document both the modified GPO setting and how you verified that indeed it is being enforced.

Running an MBSA Scan on Windows 2008 Server

16. Start the "TargetWindows02" virtual machine and login as Local Administrator:

    o Username: administrator

    o Password: ISS316Security

17. Drag and drop the downloaded MBSA installation file from the workstation to the desktop of "TargetWindows02".

NOTE: VMware tools must be installed and up to date for this to work; otherwise, you must enable a Share on the Virtual Machine Settings in VMware Player or use a USB drive to transfer the file .

---

18. Run the MBSA setup file and follow the default install steps.

19. Launch MBSA.

20. Select "Scan a Computer".

21. Remove the check mark from "Check for Security Updates" if the system does not have internet access and select "Start Scan".

Current Version Date: 05/27/2011

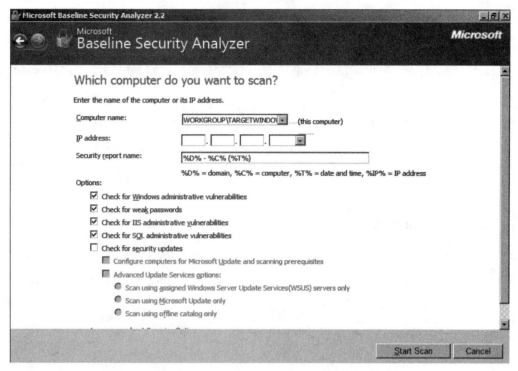

Figure 9 – Microsoft Windows Baseline Security Analyzer

22. When the scan is complete, select 'Copy to Clipboard' to save the output to the clipboard.

23. If VMware tools are installed and up to date open a new Microsoft Word document on the classroom workstation and paste the scan output into the file; otherwise, use Notepad on the virtual machine itself to paste the clipboard contents into it and save the results.

24. Save the MBSA scan output file as Lab5_MBSAScan.txt or Lab5_MBSAScan.docx.

Running an MBSA Scan on Windows XP Workstation

25. Running MBSA on a Windows XP workstation is performed by repeating the same steps taken on Windows 2008 Server

26. Start the 'Student' or 'Instructor' virtual machine and logon as Local Administrator.

    • Username: administrator

    • Password: ISS316Security

27. Drag and drop the downloaded MBSA installation file from the workstation to the desktop of your 'Student' or 'Instructor' virtual machine

28. Repeat the steps used on Windows 2008 Server to install, launch and scan MBSA on XP.

29. Save your scan results.

Current Version Date: 05/27/2011

Deliverables

Upon completion of this lab, students are required to provide the following deliverables:

1. Students should provide two documents, one in HTML format and the other in Microsoft Word format.

   • The HTML file should be a GPO report for the GPO created in this lab.

   • The Word document should contain the results of the MBSA scans.

2. Lab #5 - Assessment Questions & Answers

Evaluation Criteria and Rubrics

The following are the evaluation criteria and rubrics for Lab #5 that the students must perform:

1. Was the student able to launch GPMC, create the indicated GPO, and link the GPO to the domain? - [**20%**]

2. Was the student able to create a GPO report for the new GPO? – [**20%**]

3. Was the student able to validate that the GPO settings are in effect? – [**20%**]

4. Was the student able to launch MBSA and scan two computers to create security baselines for each one? – [**20%**]

5. Was the student able to create a scan report for each computer's MBSA scan? – [**20%**]

Current Version Date: 05/27/2011

Lab #5 – Assessment Worksheet

Course Name & Number: _____

Student Name: _____

Instructor Name: _____

Lab Due Date: _____

Overview

This lab walks the student through the steps required to define Active Directory Group Policy Objects (GPO) as well as to deploy GPOs to domain computers. It also demonstrates how to use MBSA to profile a Windows system. Group Policy Objects and vulnerability profiling are essential components to securing a Windows Active Directory environment. These two tools and methods need to be employed to provide more complete security across all of an organization's assets.

Lab #5 Assessment Questions & Answers

1. What are other available Password Policy options that could be enforce to improve security?

2. Is using the option to 'Store passwords using reversible encryption' a good security practice? Why or why not?

3. When should you enable the option to 'Store passwords using reversible encryption'?

4. Why should you use the different password policy options available (with exception to storing the password using reversible encryption)?

5. Could you perform the analysis in other computers? If so, how do you connect from the main computer?

6. What sources could you use as a source to perform the MBSA security state?

7. What does WSUS stand for and what does it do?

Current Version Date: 05/27/2011

8. What is the difference between MBSA and Microsoft Update?

9. What are some of the options that you can use when employing the MBSA tool?

10. Explain a scenario where an organization can use MBSA, WSUS and Windows Update in a combined strategy to maintain systems across an enterprise up-to-date.

Current Version Date: 05/27/2011

Laboratory #6

Lab #6: Perform a Microsoft Windows Server & Workstation Backup and Restoration

Learning Objectives and Outcomes

Upon completing this equipment-based lab, students will be able to:

- Create a Windows 2008 Server backup of a system volume drive

- Use Windows server and workstation backup and restore applications and tools

- Create backup images of a Windows 2008 Server drive volume and a Windows XP Workstation folder with data

- Restore a Windows 2008 Server drive volume from a backup image

- Restore a Windows XP Workstation folder with data files

Required Setup and Tools

The following are **required** for this equipment-based lab:

A) A classroom workstation with at least 4GB of RAM capable of supporting the removable hard drive with the VM server farm.

B) An Instructor workstation with at least 2 Gig RAM/4Gig RAM recommended that shall act as the instructor's demo lab workstation. The Instructor will display the workstation on the projector to demo the loading and configuring of the Target VMs using VMware Player.

C) Student Lab workstations will use their own VM server farm and classroom workstation. VMware Player will be used to run the Target VMs and perform the equipment-based steps.

> **NOTE:** The workstations with 4GB of RAM can support two Target VMs. Virtual machines can be Paused or Stopped when not in use in order to maximize performance. One VM at a time is recommended for a system with 2GB of RAM.

The following summarizes the setup, configuration, and equipment needed to perform Lab #6:

1. Standard classroom workstation and Virtual server farm

2. Virtual machines required for Lab #6:
   - o 'TargetWindows02': A stand-alone server Windows 2008 STD Server
     - Administrator access is as follows:
       - Username: administrator
       - Password: ISS316Security

Current Version Date: 05/27/2011

o 'Student' or ''Instructor' (or any of the provided Windows XP Workstation virtual machines): A Windows XP workstation for use by Students and Instructors

- Local Administrator access is as follows:
  - Username: administrator
  - Password: ISS316Security

Equipment-Based Lab #6 – Student Steps

For equipment-based Lab #6, students are required to perform the following steps:

1. Connect your external hard drive containing the VM Server Farm to your classroom workstation.
2. Login to the classroom workstation using your login credentials.

Install Windows Server Backup

3. Power-up and login to the 'TargetWindows02' VM as local administrator:
   - Username: administrator
   - Password: ISS316Security
4. Launch Server Manager: Start > Server Manager > Under Features click on "Add Features".
5. In the "Add Features Wizard" scroll down, click to enable "Windows Server Backup Features" and follow the instructions to perform the installation.

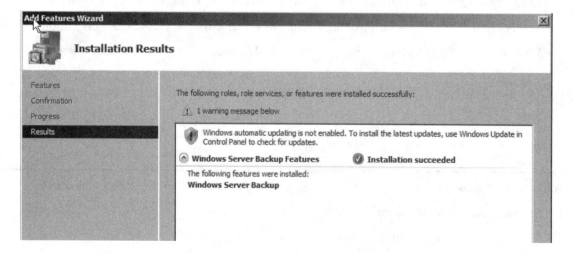

Figure 10 –Adding Windows Server Backup Utilities

Current Version Date: 05/27/2011

Backup the System Volume on a Windows 2008 Server System

6. Create a folder on the C:\ Drive of 'TargetWindows02' called "SystemBackup".

7. Right click the C:\SystemBackup folder and click "Sharing".

8. Enable Network Sharing on the Windows Server and from the drop down used to apply permissions select "Allow ALL Users" permission to the network share.

9. Launch Windows Server Backup: Start > Administrative Tools > Windows Server Backup Choose "Backup Once".

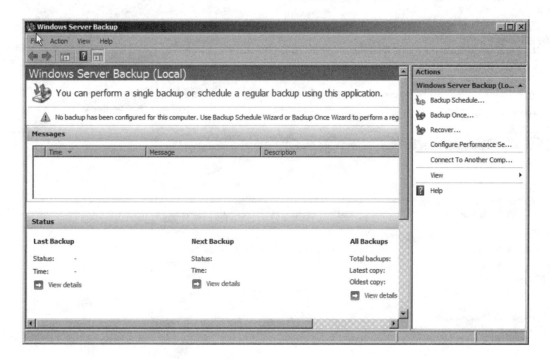

Figure 11 – Windows Server Backup Utility

10. Select "Different Options", then choose "Next".

11. Select "Custom...", then choose "Next".

12. Uncheck "all drives" and select ONLY the "D:\ volume" (which should be in the area of 55-65MB) then choose "Next".

13. Select "Remote Shared Volume:" then choose "Next" and place the following path to the shared folder: "\\TargetWindows02\SystemBackup\".

14. Choose "Back-up" to create the backup image.

15. Choose "Close" when backup is complete.

Current Version Date: 05/27/2011

Recover a System Volume from a Windows Server 2008 Backup Image

16. Log back in to the 'TargetWindows02' VM as local administrator:

    • Username: administrator

    • Password: ISS316Security

17. Launch "Windows Server Backup:": > Start > Administrative Tools > Windows Server Backup

18. Choose "Recover …".

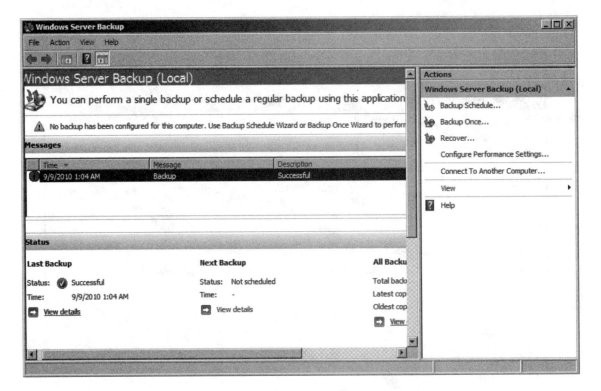

Figure 12 –Windows Server Backup Restore

19. Select "This Server" and choose "Next".

20. Select the most recent and available backup and then choose "Next" .

Current Version Date: 05/27/2011

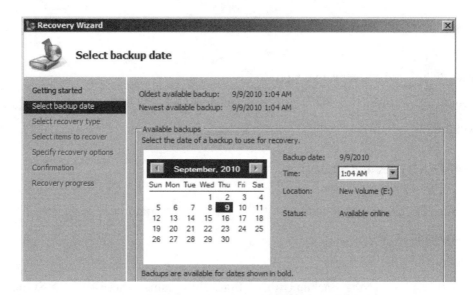

Figure 13 –Windows Server Backup Select Backup Date

21. Select "Files and Folders" and then choose "Next".

22. Expand the server item in the tree view, select "Local disk (D:)", then choose "Next".

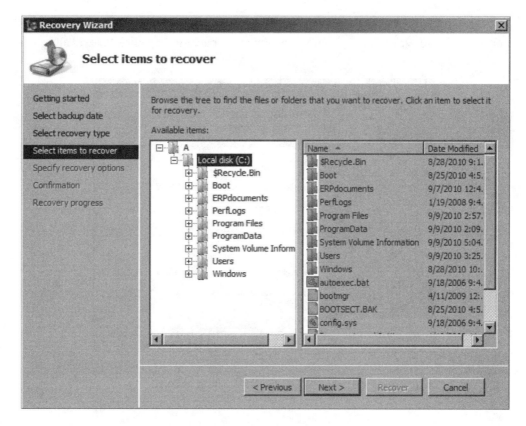

Figure 14 –Windows Server Backup Recover Menu

Current Version Date: 05/27/2011

23. Choose "Next" to select the default recovery options.

24. Review the settings then choose "Recover".

25. Choose "Close" when the recovery process is complete.

26. Reboot the "TargetWindows02" VM server and make sure the back-up and recovery/restore was successful, login, and access the D:\ drive, etc.

Backup Windows XP Files and Folders

27. Power-up and login to your "Student" VM as local administrator:
    - Username: administrator
    - Password: ISS316Security

28. Launch the "Windows XP Backup Utility": Start > Programs > Accessories > System Tools > "Backup"

29. Backup Wizard will launch.

30. Select "Backup Files and Settings" and choose "Next".

31. Select "Let Me Choose What to Backup" and choose "Next".

32. Choose the "My Documents" folder.

33. Choose "C:\" and type "Backup" for the name of the backup then click "Next" and "Finish".

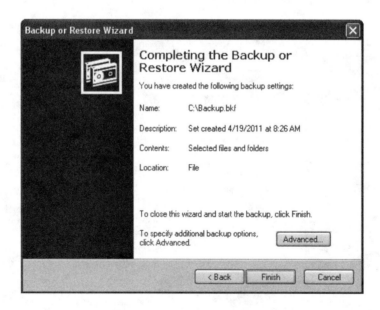

Figure 15 –Windows XP Backup Wizard

Current Version Date: 05/27/2011

34. Upon completion click on "Report" and save the output to the server's Desktop.

Figure 16 –Windows XP Backup Progress Report

35. Exit Windows Backup and Restore when backup is complete.

36. To restore the My Documents folder, run the Windows XP Backup utility once again and choose "Restore Files and Settings…" instead of Backup and locate your backup file on your server's Desktop to perform the restore.

Deliverables

Upon completion of this lab, students are required to provide the following deliverables:

1. Students should provide a document, in Microsoft Word format, containing the following content:

   • Screenshots showing each step in the Backup and Restore process for a Windows Server 2008 R2 machine (Print-Screen, Paste into MS Paint, Crop, & Cut-&-Paste into Word)

   • Screenshots showing each step in the Backup process for a Windows XP workstation (Print-Screen, Paste into MS Paint, Crop, & Cut-and-Paste into Word)

   • Describe under each screen shot, what each of the backup and restore steps perform

2. Lab #6 - Assessment Questions & Answers

Evaluation Criteria and Rubrics

The following are the evaluation criteria and rubrics for Lab #6 that the students must perform:

1. Was the student able to create a Windows 2008 Server backup of a system volume? – [**20%**]

Current Version Date: 05/27/2011

2. Was the student able to use Windows server and workstation backup and restore applications and tools? – **[20%]**

3. Was the student able to create backup images of a Windows 2008 Server drive volume and a Windows XP Workstation folder with data? – [**20%**]

4. Was the student able to restore a Windows 2008 Server drive volume from a backup image? – [**20%**]

5. Was the student able to restore a Windows XP Workstation folder with data files? – [**20%**]

Lab #6 – Assessment Worksheet

Course Name & Number: _____

Student Name: _____

Instructor Name: _____

Lab Due Date: _____

Overview

The Windows Backup utility is used as one possible method to backup and restore a Windows system. Having a sound back up and restoration strategy is a core element to being prepared to face some sort of disaster as an organization. A disaster can be as catastrophic as a natural disaster such as a hurricane or tsunami, or it can be as simple as an end user inadvertently deleting the wrong directory on a file or database server. In any case, every administrator must know how and when to properly perform backups.

Lab #6 Assessment Questions

1. What is the difference between Roles and Features in Windows Server 2008?

2. What is installed when you choose the Windows Server Backup Feature?

3. How often should servers be backed up?

4. What are the different types of backup that are perform in servers?

5. What are the primary purposes of backing up a server?

6. Besides performing and scheduling changes, what else can you do in the Windows XP Backup and Restore program? How can these applications be used as part of a Business Continuity and Disaster Recovery Plan?

7. Can you restore a server's operating system image using the restore application?

Current Version Date: 05/27/2011

8. What are the options to perform backups within Windows XP?

9. How much disk space did the backup of each the server and workstation require? Why is this important to know?

10. How long did it take to restore the Server backup image on your system and verify operation? If you had to define a recovery time objective (RTO) for performing this back-up and restore, what would you specify at an achievable goal?

Current Version Date: 05/27/2011

Laboratory #7

Lab #7: Harden a Microsoft Workstation Using Security Configuration Wizard & Manual Configurations

Learning Objectives and Outcomes

Upon completing this equipment-based lab, students will be able to:

- Define what system hardening means as it applies to Windows servers and workstations
- Harden a Windows 2008 Server network by auditing and defining security policies using the Windows Security Configuration Wizard
- Identify unnecessary roles and options configured on a Windows 2008 Server and enable additional security controls to harden the server environment within the LAN Domain
- Harden a Windows XP workstation using manual configuration of security settings within the Workstation Domain
- Review internal firewall rules on a Windows XP workstation and make recommendations to further harden the Workstation Domain

Required Setup and Tools

The following are **required** for this equipment-based lab:

A) Standard classroom workstation with at least 4GB of RAM capable of supporting the removable hard drive with the VM server farm.

B) An Instructor workstation with at least 2 Gig RAM/4Gig RAM recommended that shall act as the instructor's demo lab workstation. The Instructor will display the workstation on the projector to demo the loading and configuring of the Target VMs using VMware Player.

C) Student Lab workstations will use their own VM server farm and classroom workstation. VMware Player will be used to run the Target VMs and perform the equipment-based steps.

NOTE: The workstations with 4GB of RAM can support two Target VMs. Virtual machines can be Paused or Stopped when not in use in order to maximize performance. One VM at a time is recommended for a system with 2GB of RAM.

The following summarizes the setup, configuration, and equipment needed to perform Lab #7:

1. Standard classroom workstation and Virtual server farm.

2. Virtual machines required for Lab #7:

Current Version Date: 05/27/2011

o 'Target2k8b': A Windows 2008 domain server in the new Forest used throughout this course.

- ▪ Domain Administrator access is as follows:
- • Username: corp\administrator
- • Password: ISS316Security

o 'Student' or ''Instructor' (or any of the provided Windows XP Workstation virtual machines): A Windows XP workstation for use by Students and Instructors

- ▪ Local Administrator access is as follows:
  - o Username: administrator
  - o Password: ISS316Security

Equipment-Based Lab #7– Student Steps

For equipment-based Lab #7, students are required to perform the following steps:

1. Connect your external hard drive containing the VM Server Farm to your classroom workstation.
2. Login to the classroom workstation using your login credentials.

Use Security Configuration Wizard to harden a Windows 2008 Server R2:

3. Power-up and login to the 'TargetWindows02' VM as Local Administrator:

- • Username: administrator
- • Password: ISS316Security

4. Launch the "Security Configuration Wizard (SCW)": Start > Administrative Tools > Security Configuration Wizard.

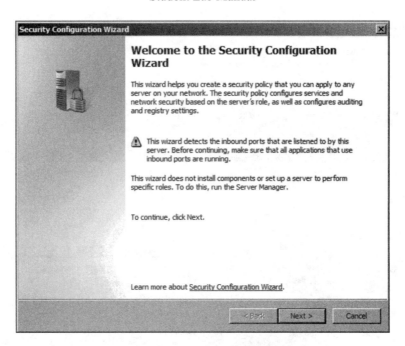

Figure 17 – Windows Security Configuration Wizard

5. Choose "Next".

6. Select "Create a New Security Policy" and choose "Next".

7. Enter the sever name and choose "Next".

8. When processing is complete if it is available select "View Configuration Database".

9. Review all the major categories and applied settings in the current Configuration Database.

10. Close the Configuration Database settings and click "Next" on the Security Configuration Wizard

11. Choose "Next" to move through the wizard pages.

12. Select the "View" drop down box and select "All Options".

13. Review all the enabled options on the server.

14. Select some additionally desired NEW options that describe the server's roles and functionality then click "Next".

15. Select "Do Not Change the Startup Mode of the Service" and click "Next".

16. Review the "Network Security Rules" enabled on the server.

17. Review the "Registry Settings", leave as default and click "Next".

18. Review the "Audit Policy", enabled desired additional settings and click "Next".

Current Version Date: 05/27/2011

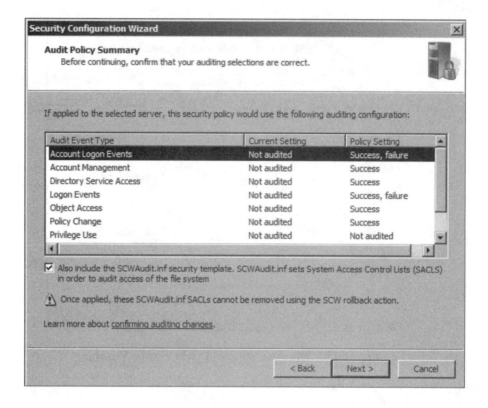

Figure 18 – Windows Security Configuration Wizard Audit Policy

19. Click "Next" on the final "Save Security Policy" dialog screen.

20. Save the new policy in the file "Securing Windows Lab #7".

21. Select "Apply Now" and choose "Next" to apply the Security Configuration Wizard suggested changes.

22. Summarize changes made by Security Configuration Wizard.

Harden a Windows XP Workstation Using Manual Configuration

23. Power-up and login to your "Student" VM as local administrator:

    - Username: administrator

    - Password: ISS316Security

24. Launch the "Windows Services" applet by right clicking the "My Computer" icon and clicking "Manage".

25. Expand "Services and Applications" in the tree view and select "Services".

26. Identify services that are not needed, disable them, and set them to "Manual".

Current Version Date: 05/27/2011

27. For more information, consult one of the following resources:

- Black Viper Windows XP Service Configurations -

  http://www.blackviper.com/Windows_7/servicecfg.htm

- Techknowl Disable unwanted Windows XP services -

  http://www.techknowl.com/2009/03/disable-unwanted-services-and-speed-up.html

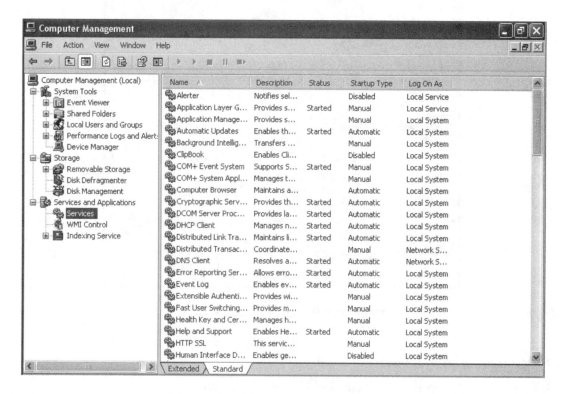

Figure 19 – Windows XP Services Applet

28. Disable unnecessary services.

- Select the desired service, open the context menu and select "Properties"

- Change "Startup Type" to "Manual" or "Disable" then choose 'OK'.

Current Version Date: 05/27/2011

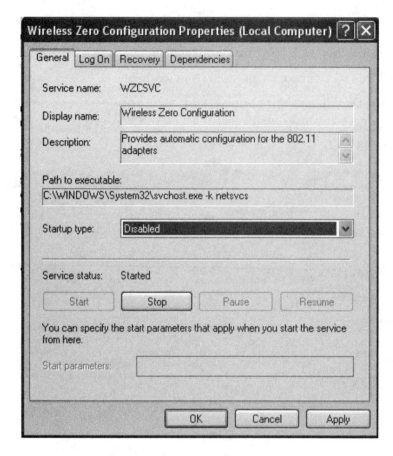

Figure 20 – Disable Windows Service

29. Document all services that are disabled.

30. Click Start > Control Panel > Windows Firewall > "Advanced".

31. Click Network Connection Settings > Settings click "Add".

32. Configure the Windows Firewall with Advanced Security firewall rules as you see fit.

33. Identify rules or exceptions that are unnecessary.

34. Uncheck and remove unnecessary rules.

35. Document all rules that are deleted or added.

Deliverables

Upon completion of lab #7, the students are required to provide the following deliverables:

1. Students should provide a document, in Microsoft Word format, containing the following content:

   • Documentation of any changes made in Security Configuration Wizard along with the reason for each change. Students should make at least six changes

Current Version Date: 05/27/2011

- A description of at least six un-needed services running on the Windows XP computer, along with a description of the suggested action that should be taken to secure each service
- A description of at least three firewall rules that should be changed on the Windows XP workstation to harden the Workstation Domain

2. Lab #7 - Assessment Questions & Answers

Evaluation Criteria and Rubrics

The following are the evaluation criteria and rubrics for Lab #7 that the students must perform:

1. Was the student able to define what system hardening means as it applies to Windows servers and workstations? – **[20%]**

2. Was the student able to harden a Windows 2008 Server network by auditing and defining security policies using the Windows Security Configuration Wizard? – **[20%]**

3. Was the student able to identify unnecessary roles and options configured on a Windows 2008 Server and enable additional security controls to harden the server environment within the LAN Domain? – **[20%]**

4. Was the student able to harden a Windows XP workstation using manual configuration of security settings within the Workstation Domain? – **[20%]**

5. Was the student able to review internal firewall rules on a Windows XP workstation and make recommendations to further harden the Workstation Domain? – **[20%]**

Current Version Date: 05/27/2011

Lab #7 – Assessment Worksheet

Course Name & Number: _____

Student Name: _____

Instructor Name: _____

Lab Due Date: _____

Overview

Windows Security Configuration Wizard (SCW) and other advanced Windows Security Features and Settings such as the Windows built-in firewall are important tools to leverage when securing a Windows system. Services that are not necessary should be disabled and set to Manual while firewall rules can be used to limit access to those services that are required for the business. With the SCW, an administrator can have the flexibility of deploying advanced security settings to the entire Active Directory Domain by leveraging the use of GPOs.

Lab #7 Assessment Questions & Answers

1. How should you apply the settings the first time you try working with SCW?

2. Why or why is it not a good option to implement this configuration from a remote location?

3. What are other ports that are normally block when using the SCW process? Identify the port number and the service or application it supports.

4. How can you run SCW in multiple servers?

5. Would the same policy work for all the servers in the domain?

6. In what Operating Systems can you use SCW?

7. What is the best practice to disable Windows XP services?

8. What is a best practice regarding disabling or enabling a Windows XP Firewall rules?

Current Version Date: 05/27/2011

9. Enable ICMP – PING filters on your internal XP firewall rules configuration to block ICMP – PING packets from hitting your XP workstation or server. How can you test that it worked properly?

10. What Windows XP Firewall policies and filters are enabled by default on the XP workstation or server?

Current Version Date: 05/27/2011

Laboratory #8

Lab #8: Apply Security Hardening on Windows Microsoft Server & Microsoft Client Applications

Learning Objectives and Outcomes

Upon completing this equipment-based lab, students will be able to:

- Identify security hardening configuration enhancements for an Internet Information Services (IIS) web services application

- Secure Internet Information Services (IIS) Server applications on Windows 2008 Server to enhance C-I-A of the web services application

- Identify security hardening configuration enhancements for a Windows XP workstation Internet Explorer browser

- Enable Internet Explorer enhanced client security settings on a Windows XP workstation to enhance C-I-A of the workstation

- Identify best practices for improving browser performance while maintaining C-I-A of the browser and workstation

Required Setup and Tools

The following are **required** for this equipment-based lab:

A) A classroom workstation with at least 4GB of RAM capable of supporting the removable hard drive with the VM server farm.

B) An Instructor workstation with at least 2 Gig RAM/4Gig RAM recommended that shall act as the instructor's demo lab workstation. The Instructor will display the workstation on the projector to demo the loading and configuring of the Target VMs using VMware Player.

C) Student Lab workstations will use their own VM server farm and classroom workstation. VMware Player will be used to run the Target VMs and perform the equipment-based steps.

NOTE: The workstations with 4GB of RAM can support two Target VMs. Virtual machines can be Paused or Stopped when not in use in order to maximize performance. One VM at a time is recommended for a system with 2GB of RAM.

Current Version Date: 05/27/2011

The following summarizes the setup, configuration, and equipment needed to perform Lab #8:

1. Standard classroom workstation and Virtual server farm.

2. Virtual machines required for Lab #8:

   o 'Target2k8b': A Windows 2008 domain server in the new Forest used throughout this course.

   ▪ Domain Administrator access is as follows:

   • Username: corp\administrator

   • Password: ISS316Security

   o 'Student' or ''Instructor' (or any of the provided Windows XP virtual machines)

   ▪ Local Administrator access is as follows:

   • Username: administrator

   • Password: ISS316Security

Equipment-Based Lab #8 – Student Steps

For equipment-based Lab #8, students are required to perform the following steps:

1. Connect your external hard drive containing the VM Server Farm to your classroom workstation.

2. Login to the classroom workstation using your login credentials.

Install and Harden Windows IIS Server

3. Logon to 'Target2k8b' as Domain Administrator:

   • Username: corp\administrator

   • Password: ISS316Security

4. Launch "Server Manager": Start > Server Manager > Under Roles click on "Add Roles", then click "Next".

5. In the Add Role Wizard, scroll down and check "Web Server (IIS)", then click "Add Required Features" and then follow the instructions to perform the installation.

6. Click Start > Administrative Tools > Internet Information Services (IIS) Manager.

7. Select the server name.

8. Double-click "Directory Browsing" and then select "Disable".

9. Double-click "Logging" and change "Directory" to use a different directory.

10. Document at least four additional changes made to IIS settings designed to harden the web server along with the reason for each change (i.e., how does it help achieve C-I-A, etc.).

Current Version Date: 05/27/2011

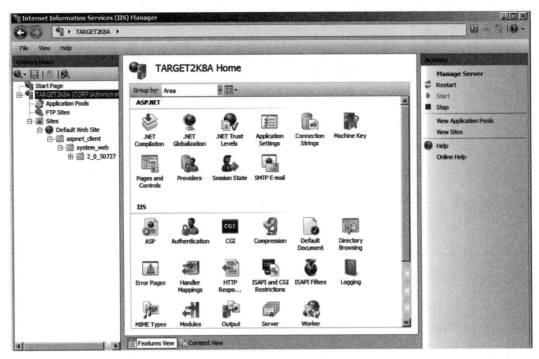

Figure 22 – IIS 7 Server Manager

Hardening Windows XP Internet Settings

11. Login to your "Student" or "Instructor" VM as local administrator:

    - Username: administrator

    - Password: ISS316Security

12. Launch "Internet Explorer": Start -> All Programs -> Internet Explorer

13. Open "Internet Options" Dialog: Tools -> Internet Options

14. Review Internet Explorer Settings for Security, Privacy and Advanced settings.

15. Suggested security hardening options:

    - Set security level of Internet zone to "High" from the "Security" tab

    - Add several websites you trust into the "Trusted Sites" list from the "Security" tab

    - Change behavior to "Prompt" for first-party and third-party cookies from the "Advanced" page (from the "Privacy" tab)

    - Check "Always Show Encoded Addresses" from the "Advanced" tab

16. Document at least four additional changes made to Internet Explorer settings designed to harden the web experience for end users along with the reason for each change.

Current Version Date: 05/27/2011

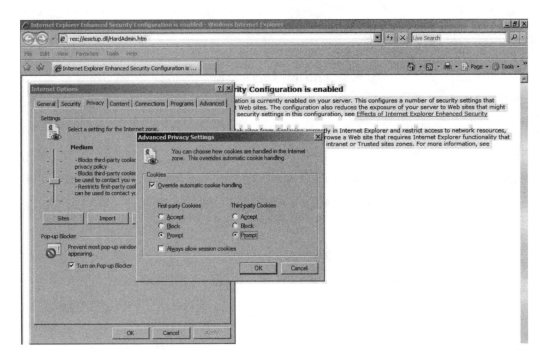

Figure 23 – Internet Explorer Privacy Settings

Deliverables

Upon completion of this lab, students are required to provide the following deliverables:

1. Lab #8 – Deliverables shall include the following:

   - Documentation of security hardening change made to the IIS web server along with a description of how that enhancement helps achieve C-I-A. Students are required to enable at least four security hardening changes.

   - A description of at least four configuration changes made to Internet Explorer to secure the web browser running on the Windows XP workstation and how that enhancement helps achieve C-I-A

2. Lab #8 - Assessment Questions & Answers

Evaluation Criteria and Rubrics

The following are the evaluation criteria and rubrics for Lab #8 that the students must perform:

1. Was the student able to identify security hardening configuration enhancements for an Internet Information Services (IIS) web services application? – [**20%**]

Current Version Date: 05/27/2011

2. Was the student able to secure Internet Information Services (IIS) Server applications on Windows 2008 Server to enhance C-I-A of the web services application? – [**20%**]

3. Was the student able to identify security hardening configuration enhancements for a Windows XP workstation Internet Explorer browser? – [**20%**]

4. Was the student able to enable Internet Explorer enhanced client security settings on a Windows XP workstation to enhance C-I-A of the workstation? – [**20%**]

5. Was the student able to identify best practices for improving browser performance while maintaining C-I-A of the browser and workstation? – [**20%**]

Lab #8 – Assessment Worksheet

Course Name & Number: _____

Student Name: _____

Instructor Name: _____

Lab Due Date: _____

Overview

It is essential to understand how to harden a Windows Server running IIS above and beyond the average Windows Server. An IIS server provides a public service that is accessible from remote machines and deserves special attention when configuring its security settings. On the client side, the Internet Explorer browser of a Windows system can execute many programs and applets that may not be desired by the end-user. They should also be locked down to provide a more secure browsing experience.

Lab #8 Assessment Questions & Answers

1. What are the steps you took to harden IIS on the Windows Sever? Explain why these steps are necessary?

2. What are the steps you took to lock down your browser? Explain why these are important security measures.

3. Which sites did you trust in IE? Why?

4. Why should you change the directory where the login is stored?

5. Should the Security updates be installed as soon as they are available?

6. With what type of privilege should services be running in the server?

7. Is it safe to assume that IE is the safest web browser since it is the most popular?

8. What other options should be checked to perform IIS hardening steps?

9. What are the most common recommendations for Windows XP users to harden their OS?

10. What are some basic recommendations for a better browser experience?

Current Version Date: 05/27/2011

Laboratory #9

Lab #9: Perform Digital Evidence Collection & Documentation Aligned with the Chain of Custody

Learning Objectives and Outcomes

Upon completing this equipment-based lab, students will be able to:

- Identify applications and tools on a Window 2008 Server R2 running IIS to perform security audits and evidence collection

- Access the Windows Event Viewer and identify failed login attempts

- Create and export a report listing the failed login attempts from Windows Event Viewer

- Access the IIS log files and identify attempts to execute cmd.exe, ftp.exe, ping, exe. net.exe or tftp.exe

- Create a report listing the attempts to execute the programs listed above and list containment and remediation steps

Required Setup and Tools

The following are **required** for this equipment-based lab:

A) A classroom workstation with at least 4GB of RAM capable of supporting the removable hard drive with the VM server farm.

B) An Instructor workstation with at least 2 Gig RAM/4Gig RAM recommended that shall act as the instructor's demo lab workstation. The Instructor will display the workstation on the projector to demo the loading and configuring of the Target VMs using VMware Player.

C) Student Lab workstations will use their own VM server farm and classroom workstation. VMware Player will be used to run the Target VMs and perform the equipment-based steps.

> **NOTE:** Workstations with 4GB of RAM can support two Target VMs along with your Student VM simultaneously. If you have 2 GB of RAM, load and run only one Target VM along with your Student VM simultaneously to maximize performance.

The following summarizes the setup, configuration, and equipment needed to perform Lab #9:

1. Standard classroom workstation and Virtual server farm.

Current Version Date: 05/27/2011

2. Virtual machines required for Lab #9:

   o 'Target2k8a': A Windows 2008 Domain Controller for a Forest used throughout this course.

      • Username: corp\administrator

      • Password: ISS316Security

   o 'Target2k8b': A Windows 2008 domain server in the new Forest used throughout this course.

      o Username: corp\administrator

      o Password: ISS316Security

Equipment-Based Lab #9 - Student Steps

For equipment-based Lab #9, students are required to perform the following steps:

1. Connect your external hard drive containing the VM Server Farm to your classroom workstation.

2. Login to the classroom workstation using your login credentials.

Detect Failed Login Attempts

3. Logon to server "Target2k8a" as Domain Administrator

   b. Username: corp\administrator

   Password: ISS316Security

4. Launch "Windows Event Viewer": Start -> Administrative Tools -> Event Viewer

5. Expand "Windows Logs" and select "Security".

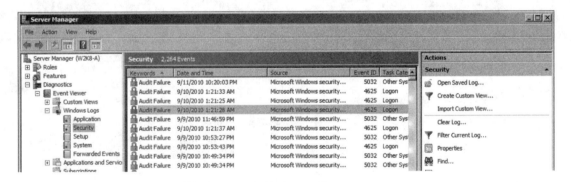

Figure 24 –Windows Event Logs

6. Select "Filter Current Log", enter "4625" in Event ID.

7. Enter "Audit Failure" in "Keywords", and then choose "OK".

8. Select "Save Filtered Log File As …" .

9. Save the log file events to a text file (change file type to txt).

Current Version Date: 05/27/2011

10. Summarize findings in a Word document and submit as a lab deliverable.

Detect IIS Attack

11. Logon to server "Target2k8b" as Domain Administrator

    a. Username: corp\administrator

    b. Password: ISS316Security

12. Open the IIS log file directory.

13. Default log folder is: C:\inetpub\logs\LogFiles\W3SVC1

14. Identify the available log files and open with Notepad or any other text editor.

15. Search for entries that contain cmd.exe, ftp.exe, ping.exe, net.exe or tftp.exe.

16. Also download SecuringWindowsLab9_IISSampleLogs.txt and analyze that log file for the same commands.

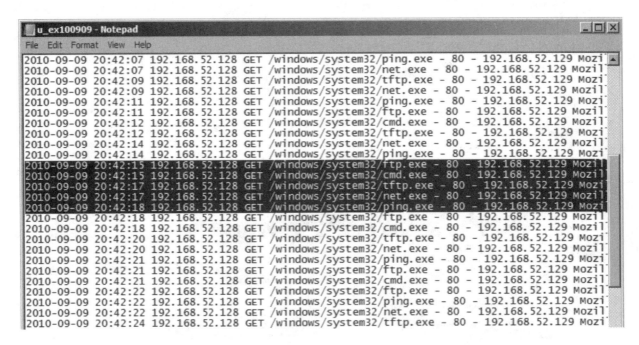

Figure 25 – Windows IIS Event Log File

17. Summarize your findings and potential remediation steps and recommendations.

Deliverables

Upon completion of this lab, students are required to provide the following deliverables:

Current Version Date: 05/27/2011

1. Students should provide a document, in Microsoft Word format, containing the following information:

   • Windows Event Log documentation of each incident detected as well as evidence supporting the incident and suggested steps to contain and eradicate the incident.

   • Windows IIS Event Log File summary of findings document.

2. Lab #9 Assessment Questions & Answers

Evaluation Criteria and Rubrics

The following are the evaluation criteria and rubrics for Lab #9 that the students must perform:

1. Was the student able to access the Windows Event Viewer and identify failed logon attempts within a 1 hour timeframe? [**20%**]

2. Was the student able to create a report listing the failed logon attempts? [**20%**]

3. Was the student able to explain your containment and remediation steps, including blocking the source computer using the Windows firewall? [**20%**]

4. Was the student able to access the IIS log files and identify attempts to execute cmd.exe, ftp.exe, ping, exe. net.exe or tftp.exe? [**20%**]

5. Was the student able to create a report listing the attempts to execute the programs listed above? [**20%**]

Current Version Date: 05/27/2011

Lab #9 – Assessment Worksheet

Course Name & Number: _____

Student Name: _____

Instructor Name: _____

Lab Due Date: _____

Overview

Being able to detect attacks based on system events within a Windows server is crucial to properly mitigating possible intrusions. This lab demonstrates how to detect failed login attempts and unauthorized access to a Windows system in the IIS logs of a running web server. It also demonstrates how to collect evidence for further analysis.

Lab #9 Assessment Questions & Answers

1. What services were attacked on the IIS server?

2. How many failed logins were detected?

3. Between what time and what time did the attacks occur?

4. What options are available to prevent brute force authentication attacks in a Windows- based domain?

5. What is an insider attacker?

6. If the attacks for Lab #9 were coming from an internal IP, would you allow the attack to continue to investigate further or stop the attack?

7. With the information provided in lab #9, if the source of the attack is external, what steps would you take to prevent reoccurrence?

8. What is the best practice to deter insiders from even thinking about executing an attack?

Current Version Date: 05/27/2011

9. Name different two types of insider attacks.

10. What is two-factor authentication?

Current Version Date: 05/27/2011

Laboratory #10

Lab #10: Perform a Security Baseline Definition Using MBSA to Harden a Microsoft Server

Learning Objectives and Outcomes

Upon completing this equipment-based lab, students will be able to:

- Identify the key features and functions of Microsoft Baseline Security Analyzer (MBSA)
- Analyze security baseline audits of Microsoft servers and workstations using MBSA
- Identify reported vulnerabilities using MBSA
- Mitigate the identified vulnerabilities and document remediation steps
- Provide security hardening and enhancements to any Windows server or workstation system

Required Setup and Tools

The following are **required** for this equipment-based lab:

A) A classroom workstation with at least 4GB of RAM capable of supporting the removable hard drive with the VM server farm.

B) An Instructor workstation with at least 2 Gig RAM/4Gig RAM recommended that shall act as the instructor's demo lab workstation. The Instructor will display the workstation on the projector to demo the loading and configuring of the Target VMs using VMware Player.

C) Student Lab workstations will use their own VM server farm and classroom workstation. VMware Player will be used to run the Target VMs and perform the equipment-based steps.

NOTE: To properly complete the **MBSA** portion of this equipment-based lab **ANY** Windows 2008 Server and Windows XP virtual machine can be used. The workstations with 4GB of RAM can run two Target VMs at once. One VM at a time is recommended for a system with 2GB of RAM.

The following summarizes the setup, configuration, and equipment needed to perform Lab #10:

1. Standard classroom workstation and the Virtual Server Farm
2. The most recent version of Microsoft Baseline Security Analyzer (MBSA) must be downloaded
3. Virtual machines required for Lab #10 are as follows:
   - "Target2k8a": A Domain Controller for a new Forest used throughout this course

Current Version Date: 05/27/2011

- Domain Name: corp.vlabs.local
- Role: Domain Controller with Active Directory and DNS Services installed
- MBSA: http://www.microsoft.com/downloads/en/details.aspx?FamilyID=b1e76bbe-71df-41e8-8b52-c871d012ba78 **must be downloaded and installed** (either from the classroom workstation BEFORE the lab or directly from the VM during the lab)
- Domain Administrator access is as follows:
  - Username: corp\administrator
  - Password: ISS316Security
  - 'Student' or ''Instructor' (or any of the provided Windows XP Workstation virtual machines): A Windows XP workstation MBSA download is also required:
    - MBSA: http://www.microsoft.com/downloads/en/details.aspx?FamilyID=b1e76bbe-71df-41e8-8b52-c871d012ba78 **must be downloaded and installed** (either from the classroom workstation BEFORE the lab or directly from the VM during the lab)
    - Local Administrator access is as follows:
      - Username: administrator
      - Password: ISS316Security

Equipment-Based Lab #10 – Student Steps

For equipment-based Lab #10, students are required to perform the following steps:

NOTE: For this lab, download from a LIVE Internet connection and install on your VM's, the latest version of Microsoft Baseline Security Analyzer for the specific OS that you have for servers and workstations, etc.

---

1. Connect your external hard drive containing the VM Server Farm to your classroom workstation.
2. Login to the classroom workstation using your login credentials.
3. Download Microsoft's Baseline Security Analyzer tools to the your classroom workstation and/or copy to your VM devices, if it is not already installed:

   http://www.microsoft.com/downloads/en/details.aspx?displaylang=en&FamilyID=02be8aee-a3b6-4d94-b1c9-4b1989e0900c

Using MBSA to Analyze and Remediate Known Software Vulnerabilities

4. Login to 'Target2k8a" as Domain Administrator:

- Username: corp\administrator

- Password: ISS316Security

5. Launch "MBSA": Start -> Microsoft Baseline Security Analyzer 2.1

NOTE: For Lab purposes, remove the check mark from "Check for Security Updates" since the lab environment will not have access to the LIVE Internet.

---

6. Select "Scan a Computer" and choose "Start Scan".

7. Review scan results and select vulnerability from each of 4 different sections .

8. Select "Result Details" and "How to Fix This" for each of the selected vulnerabilities for further details of vulnerability remediation.

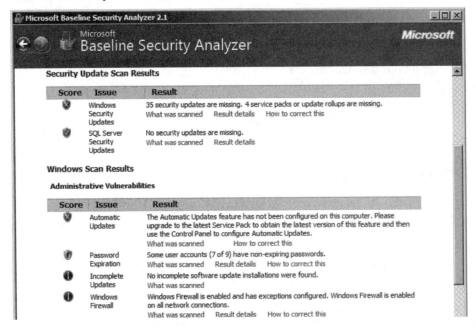

Figure 26 – Microsoft Security Baseline Analyzer

9. Mitigate each of the identified vulnerabilities and document the steps taken to identify and mitigate

Current Version Date: 05/27/2011

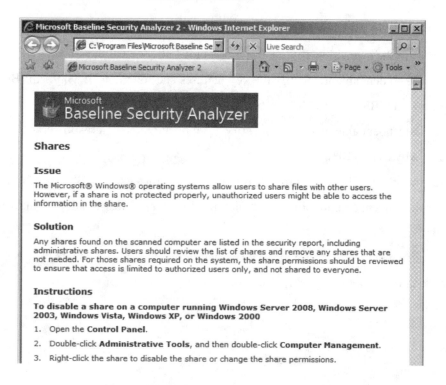

Figure 27 – MBSA Vulnerability Report

10. Re-scan your target server "Target2k8a" to verify the vulnerabilities have been mitigated.

11. Repeat these steps on either the 'Student' or 'Instructor' Windows XP virtual machine. Use MBSA to identify and then mitigate known vulnerabilities.

Deliverables

Upon completion of this lab, students are required to provide the following deliverables:

1. Students should provide a document, in Microsoft Word format, containing the following information:

   - Document each vulnerability on the Windows Server computer that MBSA identified and the student chose to mitigate. He/she should describe each vulnerability and the steps necessary to mitigate it.

   - Document each vulnerability on the Windows XP computer that MBSA identified and the student chose to mitigate. He/she should describe each vulnerability and the steps necessary to mitigate it.

2. Lab #10 - Assessment Questions & Answers

Current Version Date: 05/27/2011

Evaluation Criteria and Rubrics

The following are the evaluation criteria and rubrics for Lab #10 that the students must perform:

1. Was the student able to identify the key features and functions of Microsoft Baseline Security Analyzer (MBSA)? – [**20%**]

2. Was the student able to analyze security baseline audits of Microsoft servers and workstations using MBSA? – [**20%**]

3. Was the student able to identify reported vulnerabilities using MBSA? – [**20%**]

4. Was the student able to mitigate the identified vulnerabilities and document remediation steps? – [**20%**]

5. Was the student able to provide security hardening and enhancements to any Windows server or workstation system? – [**20%**]

Current Version Date: 05/27/2011

Lab #10 – Assessment Worksheet

Course Name & Number: _____

Student Name: _____

Instructor Name: _____

Lab Due Date: _____

Overview

The implementation of security scanners and profilers such as Microsoft's Baseline Security Analyzer (MBSA) are an important component of maintaining an up-to-date and secure Windows infrastructure.

Lab #10 Assessment Questions & Answers

1. Why is it important to run the MBSA?

2. What does an MBSA analysis look for?

3. How can MBSA be executed?

4. Does the system that is being scanned need to have access to the internet for the scan to be successful?

5. In what formats can the scan results be viewed?

6. Could you scan one computer at a time or could you perform multiple scans at a time?

7. What portion of the scan takes longer? Is it necessary to perform this scan every time?

8. Are the scans saved locally, and if so where?

9. Could you exclude patches to be scanned for?

10. Which are some of the major recommendations that you would provide to secure any Windows system?

Current Version Date: 05/27/2011